the series on school reform

Patricia A. Wasley
University of Washington

Ann Lieberman
NCREST

Joseph P. McDonald
New York University

SERIES EDITORS

the series on school reform, *continued*

Standards Reform in High-Poverty Schools

Managing Conflict
and
Building Capacity

CAROL A. BARNES

Foreword by David K. Cohen

Teachers College
Columbia University
New York and London

Published by Teachers College Press, 1234 Amsterdam Avenue, New York, NY 10027

Library of Congress Cataloging-in-Publication Data

Barnes, Carol A. (Carol Ann), 1949–
    Standards reform in high-poverty schools : managing conflict and building capacity /
Carol A. Barnes ; foreword by David K. Cohen.
        p. cm. — (The series on school reform)
    Includes bibliographical references and index.
    ISBN 0-8077-4263-5 (cloth : alk. paper) — ISBN 0-8077-4262-7 (pbk. : alk. paper)
    1. Poor children—Education (Elementary)—California—Case studies.   2. School
improvement programs—California—Case studies.   3. Education,
Elementary—Standards—California.   I. Title.   II. Series.
LC4092.C2 B37 2002
372.186'942—dc21   2002020295

ISBN 0-8077-4262-7 (paper)
ISBN 0-8077-4263-5 (cloth)

Printed on acid-free paper

Manufactured in the United States of America

09   08   07   06   05   04   03   02   8   7   6   5   4   3   2   1

This work is dedicated to the memory of Dane and Shirley.

And to the principal, staff, and students at Mission Elementary.

Contents

Foreword

Americans have been reforming public education since it began, but the last fifteen years have been unusually energetic. Schools have been criticized for concentrating on the basic skills that have been their meat and potatoes for generations. They have been attacked, by business leaders among others, not only for their lack of serious attention to the education of poor children, but also for their failure to teach them "higher-order" knowledge and skills. They have been criticized, savagely and scientifically, for their poor performance compared with that of schools in other nations; indeed, the globalization of American ideas about schooling has been a notable feature of the age. These criticisms have been part of a remarkable movement for higher academic standards, more ambitious teaching and learning, more serious efforts to boost achievement for poor children, and greater professional accountability for student performance. It has been a time of steadily increasing engagement of government and business with schools, but also, for the first time in U.S. history, of serious efforts to dismantle public education as we have known it and replace it with state supported but privately sponsored or managed schools.

The reforms have prompted an eruption of commentary, research, and argument. One broad stream of work concerns the beneficent or evil effects of reform. Most of this is little encumbered by evidence, and most of it tells a simple, single story, whether of the evils encountered in schools or the virtues of one or another rescue. Another stream consists of studies in which evidence is put, more or less honestly, in the service of established positions. A much smaller stream of work consists of studies in which authors are both dispassionate about school reforms and also deeply engaged with their effects on teachers and students. Some even report surprise at what they learned.

Dr. Carol Barnes has written such an engaged, dispassionate, and surprising book. It explores how ambitious state and federal reforms worked out for students, teachers, and administrators in one school in southern California in the early and mid-1990s. Dr. Barnes' account is not simple, but it is lucid, and deeply engaged with the clash of policy ambitions and school realities.

The reforms' ambitions had much to recommend. The state proposed to dramatically improve teaching and learning in mathematics, reading, science, social studies, among other subjects, offering one renaissance a year from Sacramento. After several decades of attention to basic skills and minimum competencies, many educators found these more ambitious reforms a welcome change, even if they were swamped by the hyperactive pace of new directions. The state enlisted school, university, and other professionals, as well as interested parents and citizens, to help write new guidance for curriculum and instruction, and to advise about revising the state assessments. The state also stimulated improved approaches to professional education for teachers already in service which would allow them to learn about the new curricula and assessments. And the state promoted the federal Title I program's intention, newly written into law in 1988, that Title I children should be taught "advanced skills," not low level remedial work.

These were noble and mostly sensible aims, and Dr. Barnes traces, with great care and clear analysis, efforts to realize them in one high-poverty school. Her book will be of interest to anyone concerned with serious efforts to improve schools, and it will be of special interest to those who are, in the wake of President George W. Bush's recent Leave No Child Behind bill, interested in the improvement of high-poverty schools.

That is because several of the central threads in her account are highly relevant to present and future school reform. California was the first state to attempt a version of the standards-based reform that Leave No Child Behind now presses with more urgency. The California reform offered ambitious guidance and encouragement for change and pressure for professional accountability. Yet as it received and welcomed that guidance, the Mission School was still more or less the school it had been before the renaissance of interest in quality schooling. Nearly all of its students were poor, and many spoke little or no English. The school was in a district that had modest fiscal resources, and that modestly supported public education. Many of the teachers were veterans who were accustomed to their district giving the school little assistance, and who though caring for the students had very limited expectations for their academic performance. Other teachers were beginners who having recently completed what passed for professional education were just beginning to learn what it might mean to be a responsible teacher of children from very poor families.

Mission School thus was the focal point of a collision between the professional habits, assumptions, and practices that arose from decades of educational indifference and neglect, on the one hand, and the aims and hopes that rode in on the crest of a sudden wave of high ambitions for public education, on the other. There were many such collisions in the last decade of the twentieth century, and we can expect many more as Leave No Child Behind moves into implementation.

In Dr. Barnes' account, high hopes and extraordinary, almost heroic efforts to respond constructively to the state reforms are mixed with the sad and often bitter legacy of educational neglect. Indeed, Mission had an inspired and energetic principal, some remarkably talented teachers, and a cadre of parents who pitched in eagerly when the school invited their help. The chapters that follow offer several compelling accounts of ambitious and engaging teaching and school leadership. Professionals in Mission worked hard to come to grips with the state's ambitious reforms, and with significant pressure for more ambitious work from the federal Title I program. But if Mission School made an extraordinary effort to respond constructively, and had much going for it, it also was a school, like many others, that the state and its district to which it belonged left more or less on its own to cope with the extraordinary new demands. It got bits of modest state and local assistance, and pressure for professional accountability, but there was nothing approaching the assistance necessary to decisively turn this school and its entire faculty around.

For however easily state policymakers might shed one policy frame for another, the school and its staff were burdened by the legacy of an unfruitful past stitched into their habits, practices, professional knowledge, social relations, and hopes. Such collisions between the human and social residue of an unfortunate past and the bright new ambitions of today's reformers are already familiar to readers, and are likely to become more familiar in the wake of Leave No Child Behind. Responding constructively to such reforms means that schools must confront themselves and deal with their own small versions of the larger social and political patterns that had helped to create the problems in the first place. These include the beliefs, which many teachers bring to school while others learn there, that poor Hispanic or African-American children cannot learn much, that less demanding work is "developmentally appropriate" for such students, and that the problem lies not in teachers' knowledge, skill, and will, but in the children and their families.

The principal and faculty of Mission engaged these and other problems, and made several major, constructive changes. Some of Dr. Barnes' classroom portraits are marvelous accounts of thoughtful and effective teaching, and student response to it. They also suggest how smart and engaged teachers can mobilize resources where others see no help and nothing to be done. The book also offers a useful account of the principal's extraordinary leadership. Yet even with such leadership and gifted teaching, some other teachers resisted the effort to raise academic performance, in part because doing so would have shaken the accommodations that they had long afforded themselves about what they might expect from their work and their students. They found it less difficult to confront the principal and the changes she sought than to confront themselves, and a battle royal ensued within the faculty. The district consequently reported that scores on tests did not improve. The tests had not been designed to track either the effects of the state reforms, or the improvements that the principal was leading, yet they were used, mindlessly, to raise questions about the school's effectiveness. That weakened both the school staff's confidence in itself, and central office support. In a sense it was no calamity, for the central office had given the school little help, but it left this unusual school and its leaders further out on the limb that the desire for serious change led them onto.

More than any other account that I know, this book respects and reflects on the complexity of schools and their history, finding grounds for both hope and dismay in one school's response to recent reforms. It confirms the importance of schools as a crucial site for efforts to improve public education, yet at the same time shows how complex schools are, how difficult it can be to move them, and how embedded their past is in present practice. The book also shows how fundamental change depends both on the work that educators do in schools and on the assistance that they need to confront the living legacies of the past and to learn to devise new practices, social relations, and organization. Carol Barnes wisely situates the Mission School's struggle to improve in the long U.S. history of such efforts, connecting this school's struggles with those of the past, as well as with the intellectual and political wars that Americans have waged over their schools. It offers the best portrait that I know of how difficult it can be to turn a school around, and *why* it is difficult. Perhaps most important, it offers a vital insight into how the battles that Americans fight, among themselves, on the larger stages of public life, also must be fought and won in the smaller worlds of public schools, with and among those who work there if there is to be much hope of making our schools better places for teachers to work and for poor children to learn.

David K. Cohen
John Dewey Professor of Education
Professor of Public Policy
The University of Michigan

Preface

In this book I tried to illustrate something about the nature of education reform in America using the experience of people in schools as they struggled to both maintain and transform their professional responsibilities. In part, I directed the view of reform in the book to today's teachers and students of policy, as well as to the policy conversation in which I once participated. From that experience, I offer this observation: While state and federal policy planners often have honorable motives for wanting to "shake up" the education system, the advantage of hindsight and years of study in schools have convinced me that many of their "solutions" are naïve, or at worst, arrogant. This book brings the voices of people in one school to the "policy table" at which so many sit with little understanding of the other realities involved in their reform strategies—even those strategies that are well reasoned and based on the authority of research. While I have tried to be balanced, my sympathies were often with the people I observed for several years as they struggled in the "trenches" of educational reform. The view here pulls apart and examines their world, but the totality of that world was more than its parts.

Acknowledgments

My research at Mission Elementary emerged from the Education Policy and Practice Study (EPPS), which was sponsored in part by a grant from the U.S. Office of Educational Research and Improvement to the Consortium for Policy Research in Education, and by grants from the Carnegie Corporation of New York and The Pew Charitable Trusts. I have benefited a great deal from the time, energy, careful readings, advice, and friendship of researchers on the EPPS project—the principal investigators, and others. I am grateful to David Cohen for his years of guidance as my advisor, supporter, and most exacting critic. I am indebted also to Penelope Peterson, Suzanne Wilson, and Deborah Ball. They served as the principal investigators for the EPPS at Michigan State University. I was extremely fortunate to participate in the vital research community they created there. Sue Poppink, Steve Mattson, Jennifer Norman, Jeremy Price, James Spillane, Ruth Heaton, Nancy Jennings, S. G. Grant, and Jim Bowker contributed a great deal to the intellectual excellence of that community as well. Kara Suzuka, Dirck Roosevelt, and Sarah Theule-Lubienski were important and thoughtful companions with whom I consulted during the year I was poring over data. Justin Crumbaugh, now a graduate student in Spanish literature, provided me with the exemplary support I needed to interpret conversations in Spanish during my fieldwork. Finally, Gary Sykes, Jay Featherstone, David Labaree, Steve Weiland, and Peter Vinten-Johansen all provided helpful advice during the years I was immersed in studying Mission Elementary School. I am grateful for their wide-ranging knowledge. While many of these people contributed to my thinking, the views expressed in this study are my own and not necessarily shared by the granting agencies, other project researchers, or my mentors at Michigan State University.

The teachers and school leaders who inhabit this book were not primarily focused on making sense of policy. Rather, they were trying to construct a meaningful life, and a better world for their students. I thank Jay Featherstone for reminding me of this point. And, I want to thank the principal, staff, and students at Mission Elementary for welcoming me into their world.

CHAPTER 1

Mission Elementary: An Introduction

In the fall of 1994, Laura Mather, the principal of Mission Elementary, was in tears, her head resting on the desk in her office.* It had been a long day ending in emotional confrontation with her staff. A series of after-school "across grade" meetings had erupted in name-calling due to a new school-wide Title I plan that sought to encourage the staff to take mutual obligation for a clearer and more focused school mission. Kindergarten teachers had filed a grievance with the union over details in the new plan. One teacher, Anita Lorenz, broke rank with the others; and this evening another teacher called her a wimp for doing so. Ruth Linn, the school's bilingual mentor, heard about the meeting from Lorenz, who told her "it was brutal, really brutal."

For some time Mather had worried that teachers—especially the primary grade teachers—were working too independently. Of the kindergarten teachers, she said: "They need to come into [the first grade classroom] to see how those kids function and what is expected of them and everybody else in [first grade]." Mather was trying to forge a common sense of responsibility for student work among her teachers, but admitted it hadn't been easy. Louise James, Mather's friend and Title I assistant, concurred. She remembered the November meeting that ended with Mather in tears:

> We all stayed [late] . . . and the whole discussion disintegrated. All of a sudden they were no longer talking about programs. They were talking about and bashing people. . . . And there were . . . people with feelings hurt, and tears; there were lots of tears. It was awful. It was awful.

Conflict had erupted over new school goals and work norms, but there were other sources of conflict on Laura Mather's mind as well: She felt under siege by parents who objected to a new "learning assessment" the district had piloted that past spring. Mather reported a father had told her "the CLAS [Cali-

---

*All names used in this study—people, school, and district—are pseudonyms.

fornia Learning Assessment System] test is just another way for the federal government to strip us of our individualism." Mather worried, too, about heightened hostilities that were developing between the Spanish-speaking students and the English-speaking students. A few months before, Mexican American parents had accused her of racism, of allowing Anglo children to beat up and call their children names. Some parents had also complained that their children were not learning to speak English soon enough because of the district's "late exit" bilingual program. She and her staff were having second thoughts about that project which provided native language instruction in core subjects such as math and language arts. Meanwhile, the morning traffic in the parking lot was causing problems, and the district psychologist had reported that one of the new students at Mission was likely homicidal—perhaps due to the severe beatings he had suffered at home. Those troubles, along with the graffiti problem on the school walls (which Mather suspected a gang of junior high boys of doing) meant another early morning in the parking lot ensuring students' safe arrival and overseeing cleanup. Laura Mather was tired, but determined.

The conflict that Laura Mather and her staff was trying to manage at Mission Elementary in the fall of 1994 was in part bound up with an unprecedented education reform calling for demanding instruction and curriculum for all children, including America's poor, minority students. That call—together with the press for the professional collaboration of educators around a more coherent, systemic, reform strategy—took place in California, then at the federal level, in the midst of political conflict and long-standing disagreement over educational goals and means. While schools such as Mission Elementary are becoming increasingly common in the United States, little has been reported about how the reforms have fared in these "high-poverty" schools. This book reports on the "implementation" or "enactment" of one of the most ambitious education reform attempts in recent history, in one such school. Moreover, it does so in California, a state that was in some respects ahead of the federal government's Goals 2000 and Title I reforms.

The story of Mission Elementary provides a detailed, ground-level perspective on what happens when unprecedented reforms intended to improve the quality and equity of instruction for poor children, encounter the schools they seek to improve. That perspective on reform—from the work of small groups of students and teachers, to the problem of changing classroom instruction, to the interaction of teachers and administrators in the school as a whole—shows that the fate of the curriculum standards depended on the enactors' capacity to understand and respond to demanding reform ideas in the midst of conflict and inconsistency. This book explores what the staff brought to the enactment task and what they were able to learn. It considers what conventional resources they had, how they used them, and the "social capital" they were able to create from those resources—all the while coping with the conflict inherent in American education.

The recent reforms didn't eliminate competing traditions or inherited ideas about teaching, curriculum, and the purposes of schools in Mission Elementary, the school's district, the state, or the nation. A strong tradition of teacher autonomy is one such competing convention; inherited ideas about basic skill instruction and testing is another. In California and in the district where Mission Elementary is located, there were also battles over the role of language in public education, and controversy over the state or local role in educating poor, immigrant children. Likewise, long-standing disputes—about the nature of learning, the problem of low achievement among poor, language-minority children, and the place of diverse cultures within American society—shaped the reforms' larger historical context. Mission Elementary's staff and students not only interacted with, but in part embodied the disputes in this larger historical, national, state, and local context.

THE SCHOOL

Traveling inland to Mission Elementary with the morning sun bathing the coastal foothills in bright light, one can almost imagine the impressive expanse of California land as it might have looked years ago. The hills, stretching as far as the eye can see under a cobalt blue sky, veer up from the Pacific Ocean to give the area a prodigious look and feel. Just over 150 years ago, this part of the United States was the Republic of Mexico. But today, telephone wires cut across the still blue sky, and small cities or incorporated villages have covered the land from the ocean to the street where Mission Elementary sits. Now the Maracas United School District (MUSD) covers 38 square miles of this region, and includes parts of four cities along with a considerable portion of the urban sprawl between them. By the time this research was conducted, seven new schools had opened there to accommodate the rapidly growing population in the area. According to district officials, much of that growth had been from children arriving from Mexico. In the 1991–1992 school year, an MUSD voluntary desegregation plan moved children from Santa Maria —a barrio school where 88% of the children enrolled were Mexican American and 70% spoke limited English—to other district schools. Mission Elementary was one of three schools that received the greatest number of poor children—a number that has grown since.

Mobile home parks cramped with old trailers, many in disrepair, line one side of Mission Boulevard, the road leading up to Mission Elementary School. Further down the road there are small houses pressed together, each with its parcel of land covered with bougainvillea and other brilliant flowers. Further still, where the boulevard meets the crest of the hills surrounding Mission Elementary, there are larger homes and lots signaling the comfortable socioeconomic status of their occupants. On a typical day, a visitor to the school would find the school's principal, Laura Mather, standing in front greeting students as they made their way to morning class. Due to budget cuts, only one bus traveled to Mission Elementary. As a result cars congested the parking lot, pulling in and out to drop off children whose complexions ranged from deepest browns to palest beige. Glancing around at the flurry of activity, a visitor would be quick to note the children's racial and ethnic diversity as they gathered in groups to talk or laugh.

Like many schools in California, Mission Elementary was overcrowded; and like many school staffs, Mission's faced enormous problems in its work of educating poor, limited English speaking, minority children. The school was open year round and enrolled nearly 950 children. More than 70% of those children were poor, 68% were minority, many of them Mexican American immigrants who spoke limited English. The staff reported that many of their students were transient. Further, some of the children who arrived at this school had not passed the first grade in Mexico, though they were 10 or 11 years old. The staff also reported that some of these young children arrived at school with their bodies and souls in need of repair: They were on various occasions hungry, tired, physically ill, emotionally troubled, or otherwise abused by their living conditions.

Indeed, Laura Mather invested a considerable amount of her personal and professional time directly in Mission's students: Their academic work and their welfare were important concerns to her. She was their protector, defender, disciplinarian, fund-raiser, leader, and teacher. Sometimes she despaired over them. She was frustrated to tears on more than one occasion because she was unable to protect her students from the circumstances of their lives. For example, Mather reported handing one kindergarten girl over to her mother who arrived at school screaming due to various drugs she had consumed. Though Mather called the police, to her dismay the child still had to be released to the mother's care. A fourth-grade boy's anger became unmanageable in the classroom. He was sent to California to live with his maternal grandparents after suffering from severe beatings from his parents in North Carolina. Another boy whose instruction I followed for 2 years was living in a foster home because his mother was in jail for murder. Despite setbacks, Mather appeared tireless in her determination to help Mission's students overcome their life circumstances and achieve academically.

Thus, if Mission Elementary is typical of many schools that embody America's educational challenges, Laura Mather and her leadership team were somewhat unusual—not only in the energy they dedicated to the welfare of their students, but in their commitment to Mission's continuing improvement.

Since her arrival at the school in 1988, Mather had worked to improve it by hiring new, reform-minded staff, by encouraging new ideas, by recruiting parent volunteers, raising funds for refurbishing buildings, and so on. Due in large part to Mather and her leadership team, Mission Elementary was a caring and interesting place to be: Children had their breakfast and lunch on picnic tables framed by a mural of an underwater scene, a sunroof, and an outdoor walkway. A parent volunteer painted the mural. The school was open early and remained open late for those children who needed a place to stay. There were educational games and books available for early arrivals. The children at Mission Elementary planted, tended, harvested, and wrote about their school garden, which was quite lovely. A science teacher volunteered his time to design and help develop the garden.

Moreover, many children appeared to be growing adept at using the computers in the new computer lab for a variety of purposes—one of which was to hone problem-solving skills. Mission's students spent time in the science laboratory, "conducting experiments, doing science," just as the state science framework suggested they should. Many of the children were learning to play a Mariachi instrument, and nearly every recess as they practiced, a visitor could hear the tinkling sounds of mandolin music drifting through the school. One of Mission's teachers, whose Irish family has long played in a Mariachi band, volunteered his time to teach any child who wanted to learn. All the children took part in dramatic performances and other creative endeavors. I observed the English-speaking children performing in a skit speaking only Spanish. Most Spanish speakers understood and used some English.

While there were fights, children were also willing and able to work in cooperative groups (one aspect of the instructional reform), and to help each other in the spirit of the "conflict resolution" program the staff had adopted. For example, Ana, one little girl I observed for 2 years, was especially small for her age. Occasionally children would taunt her on the playground because of her speech impediment. But she had many protectors at Mission Elementary: children who stood up for her, children who wrote her letters expressing their friendship during "free writing time," children who helped her with her academic work.

Laura Mather and her leadership team—made up mostly of staff Mather had recently hired—knew Ana. They knew about her history in Mexico. The school's leadership knew that Ana's friend Nan, another Title I student, missed a lot of school. Her mother sometimes took Nan out of school on Mondays and Fridays when she cleaned other people's houses. But Mather was also aware that Nan was doing better than she had the year before and believed it was due to special tutoring she received from Monique Ponds, Mission's bilingual Title I teacher. Monique was one of several newly hired teachers who appeared especially dedicated to improving the academic performance of

Mission's students. Mather knew all her students by name. She and her staff—one classroom teacher at a time—organized daylong meetings centered on individual children. They borrowed the idea from the special education process. The speech therapist was at Ana's meeting, as were her teacher and her mother. Laura Mather had attended them for almost every student; a central feature of the discussions was how to improve the students' academic work.

THE REFORM AND ITS ENVIRONMENTS

In the fall of 1994, the work of school improvement involved coping with considerable conflict, as the opening vignette showed. The conflict at Mission Elementary that fall was rooted in part in the staff's continuing response to ambitious academic reforms that were first pressed by the 1988 Hawkins-Stafford amendments to Chapter 1 (now Title I) of the Elementary and Secondary Education Act (ESEA). The amendments called for teaching advanced intellectual skills to all children, and in doing so contradicted at least 2 decades of policy and practice that had encouraged remedial work—improving basic skills—for children disadvantaged by poverty. Congress expanded the ideals in the 1988 amendments in 1994 when it reauthorized Title I and linked it to a new federal initiative, Goals 2000. Those two policies sought to encourage coherent curricular frameworks and accountability systems that would press the country's schools further in the direction of high standards of intellectual achievement for all children.

Thus, the reauthorized Title I renewed the press for "school-wide projects" which grew in part out of research suggesting that professional school norms can improve achievement (Pechman & Fiester, 1994). Such norms include a cohesive, collegial community in which teachers take mutual responsibility for students' high academic achievement. School staffs forge shared goals through deliberation and negotiation of defensible practices (Carnegie Forum on Education and the Economy, 1986; Holmes Group, 1990; Little, 1990; Newmann & Wehlage, 1995; Purkey & Smith, 1983; Sykes, 1990). *Coherence*, professional *collaboration*, and intellectually rigorous academic *standards for all students*: these were the themes in the cluster of reforms that were making their way into Mission Elementary during the course of my time there—from the fall of 1993 to the spring of 1995.

State Leadership and Reform

The fact that those reform ideas were in the air at Mission Elementary is not surprising, for California had been one state leading the standards reform for all students. For example, a 1988 California State Department program advisory based on then new amendments to Chapter 1 (now Title I) repeatedly emphasized that all children were entitled to an intellectually challenging education. The advisory rejected "pull-out" strategies that focused on reme-dial instruction of low-level skills, claiming that such strategies isolated chil-dren from higher-achieving peers. It favored "regular classroom" instruction that emphasized thinking and communicating about "rich content."

California's mathematics and language arts curriculum frameworks also called for higher standards for all children. The 1988 *English-Language Arts Model Curriculum Guide* stressed engaging all California students—those "from widely diverse ethnic, racial, linguistic, and economic backgrounds"— in "disciplined academic study" (California State Department of Education, 1988, p. v). Since at least 1985, the mathematics framework has also called for intellectually ambitious instruction for all children (Webb, 1993). Then California State Superintendent William Honig wanted the 1985 Mathemat-ics Framework to outline an inclusive vision of rigorous mathematics educa-tion. On that point he said: "Every student can enjoy and use mathematics to real advantage and . . . the power of mathematical thinking is not reserved for only an academic elite" (Webb, p. 126).

By early 1995, California's new state superintendent Delaine Eastin pressed the ideas in Goals 2000 and the reauthorized Title I in regional meetings orga-nized for local educators. Laura Mather attended one such meeting and returned with a memorandum—"Goals 2000 Request for Applications" (March 1, 1995)— that the state department of education was distributing. The memorandum called for local applicants to "thoughtfully consider . . . how greater coherency can be created" (p. 3). Criteria for judging plans included evidence of a "shared vision of teaching and learning that is centered around high standards of achieve-ment for every student." And they included "a commitment to working in . . . a collaborative manner throughout the change effort" (p. 16).

Political Controversies and Conflicting Traditions

But a turbulent political environment surrounded and permeated Mission Elementary school as educators there tried to learn about these new ideas calling for coherence, professional collaboration, and complex intellectual achievement for all children. And the recent reform is one of many to have accumulated in an education system that offers an array of competing pro-gram ideas from many countervailing sources. In California and at the MUSD, there were policy debates over the goals of education and popular resistance to the reform ideas. In December 1992, several new conservative Christian board members were elected in the MUSD, giving the majority on the five-member board to that group. In part, the new members represented citi-zen groups who were arguing that the reforms pressing for critical thinking undermined religious and parental authority. The call for educating all children to high intellectual standards was, according to some, an infringement on individualism.

The CLAS in particular became the center of a great deal of controversy and some popular resistance in southern California: thus Laura Mather's concern, sketched in the opening vignette, over the just-emerging parental resistance to the CLAS in the fall of 1994. The fledgling instrument was California's attempt at developing a more authentic statewide assessment in alignment with their intellectually demanding curriculum frameworks. It included open-ended problems that pressed students to engage in considerable writing and thinking, and which sometimes required them to justify their answers through reasoning. But some parents in the MUSD whose children attended Mission Elementary were worried that the CLAS was an instrument for violating family privacy, undermining authority, and for stamping out individual achievement and academic excellence. Mather had been reassuring parents but reported being unable to convince some of them. Meanwhile, the district hired a teacher who was a member of the conservative Christian community to act as the "parent liaison" for concerns about the CLAS.

But that wasn't the only conflict surrounding the CLAS: The MUSD required schools to give their students the California Test of Basic Skills (CTBS), a standardized basic skills test, as well as the CLAS. One reason was that federal programs—Title I of the ESEA, for example—still required such a measure of student progress until the 1994–1995 school year. By that time, the CLAS was under attack for everything from invading privacy to producing invalid results. But different assumptions about teaching and learning inform the CLAS and CTBS. The central tendency of the CLAS was to reward independent thought and complex performances demonstrating students' understanding of subject matter aligned with the reform curriculum. The CTBS expected rapid selection of "factual" answers which drew on more basic levels of cognitive functioning—not necessarily aligned with reform content.

The assumptions informing the CTBS represent one set of inherited traditions that competed with the reforms; strong norms of teacher autonomy represent another. Where instructional preferences are at stake, teachers have long been committed to a culture of privacy and individualism, not collaboration (Little, 1990; Lortie, 1975; Sykes, 1990). Some of the school-level conflict that erupted at Mission was rooted in Laura Mather's attempt to open her teachers' personal, instructional choices to collegial scrutiny. Such scrutiny conflicted quite dramatically with traditional norms of teacher autonomy. And, the press for new school norms uncovered strong staff disagreement as well as charged public debate over instructional goals and means. Meanwhile, two third-grade teachers—the no-nonsense Kate Jones and her partner Alice Michiels, who had been working as a team for some time—were arguing over the assumptions in the CTBS and the CLAS, even before the school's attempt to reach some agreement on school-wide goals.

Conflicting opinion over educating Mexican immigrant children in California schools confounded the instruction and assessment debates, and added to the political turmoil in the state as well as in the school. At Mission, teachers held conflicting opinions about the district's "late exit" bilingual policy; and they disagreed over the meaning of equitable standards as those standards were entangled with language. Juan Ramirez, a young, first-generation Mexican American teacher, accused another teacher of not holding high enough standards for Spanish-speaking children and of using a "developmental" approach as "an excuse for not teaching." Laura Mather worried that language was creating conflict between Spanish-speaking children and English-speaking children. At the district level, several Maracas school board members told a large crowd at one of their meetings in the spring of 1994 that funds for bilingual education should be used for the "real Maracas students"—that is, those who speak English and who were born in the United States.

Such local controversy reflected in part the state turmoil over educating immigrants. For example, in an unusual move, the state senate challenged one of then governor Pete Wilson's state board of education appointments because he had supported an assembly bill intended to prevent undocumented migrant children from attending public schools. The bill drew much testimony, both pro and con. Some Hispanic lawmakers accused the legislation and the Republicans of immigrant bashing. But a parent told the assembly committee that his children's education was in jeopardy because the Spanish-speaking children of undocumented migrant workers dominated their school. A teacher testified that English-speaking teachers with years of seniority were losing their jobs, while junior bilingual teachers kept theirs. Supporters said it would save millions of dollars; opponents said it would punish innocent children. The Education Committee rejected the bill by an 8–3 vote but a statewide referendum with similar intent—Proposition 187—passed by quite a majority in November 1994.

Not only were Mather and her staff trying to make sense of reforms, in this context of conflicting traditions and political controversy, but they were doing so with dwindling resources. The arguments that staff at Mission were having in the fall of 1994 over badly needed categorical resources were in part a reflection of the problem of repeated budget cuts at the MUSD. At the time of my research, simultaneous limits on local and state spending for education, along with a state recession, had left many California schools—Mission Elementary among them—overcrowded and in need of repair. At Mission, burgeoning enrollments and funding cuts had created large teacher-pupil ratios, traffic congestion, and time-consuming administrative tasks for Mission's staff. Thus dwindling resources and political controversy, along with disagreements over instruction, curriculum, and assessments, contributed to the environment in which staff at Mission Elementary School were trying to work out new ideas about schooling.

Historical School Reform Context

But the reforms at Mission were also unfolding within a larger historical context of social science debate and political action.* For example, the complex, sometimes contradictory, assumptions underlying policies designed to remedy the effects of disadvantage have interacted over time with competing assumptions about teaching, learning, and assessment. Many of these assumptions had accumulated in and around Mission Elementary, clustered in categorical programs or related policies. To explore the standards reforms and the question of how Mission's staff enacted them in their daily work, this book focuses on three key policy categories: Title I of the ESEA; Title VII of the ESEA (Bilingual Education); and curriculum reforms instantiated in the California curriculum frameworks, the CLAS, or other state reform instruments. Thus, long-standing debates about the nature of cognition, the problem of low achievement among poor and language-minority children, and the place of diverse languages or cultures within American society are salient here.

The California curriculum frameworks drew on the premises and evidence in *Becoming a Nation of Readers* (Anderson, Hiebert, Scott, & Wilkinson, 1985), a report surveying at least 2 decades of research on reading, as well as those in other documents put out by a series of professional standards projects. *Becoming a Nation of Readers* called for higher standards of literacy and declared reading to be a matter of making sense of "rich" texts. The report made a "constructivist" argument: "Text comprehension depends upon a reader's prior knowledge, experience and attitudes; meaning is constructed as a reader links what he reads to what he knows" (p. vi).

These comments were in part a reflection of the growing number of cognitive scientists who took learning to be an active matter of making sense of the world, rather than passively responding to it.

Such arguments about the nature of learning and mind contrast quite dramatically with the premises of the educational psychology that had been prominent in America for almost a century. Edward Lee Thorndike shaped the practices of a majority of teachers and school staff for decades during his years at Columbia University's Teachers College (Joncich, 1962). Thorndike (and others) cast learning as behavior, not as an active mental process of

---

*The material in this section was informed by work I did with David K. Cohen and supported by the Carnegie Corporation of New York.

making sense. The learner was a responder, not a creator of meaning. Motivation for learning was external, not located internally, in the questions and experiences of the learner.

For years Thorndike had also argued that curriculum ought to be specialized, based on differences in the inherent capacity of children; and that attempts to bring all students up to one standard were inappropriate, if not impossible:

> It would be wasteful for a man of a certain original nature and training to be taught to manipulate logarithms. . . . Here, as everywhere . . . the persons to be educated decide in part what the proximate aims of education should be. (Thorndike, 1912, p. 40)

In Thorndike's vision, academic goals were far from standard; rather, social engineers would construct them based on individual differences. In the 50s, 60s, and 70s, Robert Gagne, Benjamin Bloom, and other theorists expanded on and modified some of Thorndike's themes arguing for sequential instruction based on differences in student "pace," rather than inherent capacity. But both men argued that the hierarchical structure of learning or knowledge ought to be the organizing principle for instruction, and that simple concrete skills formed the basis for increasingly more complex, abstract ones (Bloom, 1956; Bloom, Hastings, & Madaus, 1971; Gagne, 1965/1970).

The reform ideas that had made their way into Mission Elementary competed with this conception of teaching and learning. The big ideas in the new wave of reform grew in part out of cognitive conceptions of learning built on the seminal work of Jean Piaget, Lev Vygotsky, John Dewey (1916/1966), and a few others. Piaget argued that children make sense of their world by constructing their understanding over time, building on what they already know. Vygotsky placed culture and social interaction with others—not the individual—at the center of human development, but maintained the idea that humans construct meaning. These men and Dewey were followed by American developmental or cognitive psychologists—Jerome Bruner, prominent among them—who reinforced the importance of "meaning" and culture to mind and learning (Bruner, 1983, 1990).

Those reform ideas were unusual in recent history because they suggested that basic skills and complex thinking could be learned simultaneously rather than hierarchically. Subject matter complexity could be reduced through social interaction or "scaffolding" rather than by doling out knowledge to students in discrete bits as popular theories of learning had implied. Indeed, in cognitive conceptions, the purpose of any genuine learning was understanding, which requires complex and critical thought based on prior experience and new information.

But as Title I of the ESEA was taking shape in the 1960s, it followed from the prevailing arguments about the nature of learning and poverty that poor children should compensate for learning deficits through remedial work; that is, they should begin at the bottom of a skills hierarchy, with isolated bits of information and discrete, low-level tasks. Title I—the heart of the federal government's educational reform effort at that time—was informed in part by theories that defined the problem of persistent, low academic achievement by poor children as a matter of "cultural deprivation" (Lewis, 1959; Riessman, 1962). Children receiving Title I help were pulled out of classrooms—in part as a tracking mechanism for federal dollars—to receive their special "compensatory instruction." Following the logic of the arguments just sketched, that instruction was most often drill and practice in low-level skills (Allington, 1991; Odden, 1991; Turnbull, 1990).

In the early 70s, some social scientists and minority activists resisted the assumptions underlying compensatory education. Baratz and Baratz (1970), for example, blamed social scientists and the Title I advocates for failing to frame the problem properly, and thus offering the wrong remedy: "Ethnocentric liberal ideology undergirding social intervention programs denies cultural differences" (p. 30). They wanted schools to use "multicultural" materials, tests, and instructional strategies—strategies that used the children's existing culture and language to teach them new ones. Community activists were making similar indictments and calling for similar strategies (Carmichael & Hamilton, 1967). Here, cultural difference rather than deficiency was the key assumption explaining the problem of low achievement among poor, minority children.

That idea—how or whether educators ought to address cultural differences—was the center of a political dispute in the MUSD when I began my research. Likewise, it played an important role at the inception of the Bilingual Education Act in this country. After congressional hearings during which the idea of validating cultural differences was a powerful theme, Lyndon Johnson signed that act into law in 1968. Diane Ravitch (1983) argues that the purposes of bilingual education were hugely controversial. Support for cultural and language maintenance came from bilingual educators and ethnic group leaders, while members of Congress and federal administrators wanted to help students adapt to the mainstream of American life by teaching them to speak English. Such public debates over language have been prominent in California, at least since the Progressive Era when the West was opened up by the railroads in the 1880s. At that time, non-Spanish-speaking "immigrants" began pouring in from the Eastern United States, setting off a long-standing argument about the "official" language of the area (Acuña, 1988; Raftery, 1992).

Thus, the call for intellectually rigorous instruction for all children was unprecedented in recent history. Opinion was and is still divided over what sort of instruction is most effective for all children, but especially children disadvantaged by the effects of social and economic circumstances. Opinion is divided over whether or not there are effects. Nevertheless, for years attempts to improve the achievement of poor children have most often included remedial instruction of basic skills. The newer curriculum policies not only challenged the assumptions informing remedial education, but they contradicted many of the big ideas in a long tradition of teaching, learning, and knowing in this country.

Like many American schools, Mission Elementary embodied the disputes as well as the challenges that are central concerns of the reforms. Given the historical context and reform environment just sketched, any response to the call for intellectually demanding instruction for all children would be set in a sea of diverse and conflicting opinion. How did this school—its staff, leadership, and students—typical of many American schools, respond to curriculum reform calling for rigorous academic standards for all children? How did such reforms and the staff's response interact with other programs in the school; that is, those designed to remedy the effects of social, economic, or linguistic disadvantage? What happens when these policy and program ideas meet in a school enrolling many poor, limited-English-speaking children?

CONFLICT AND CAPACITY

The fate of curriculum reform in this school depended on the staff's capacity to understand and enact complex instructional or organizational change while coping with considerable conflict in policy goals, in professional commitments, and in relationships. Mission Elementary's story illuminates how conflict was not only an integral part of the "implementation" or "enactment" process, but how it contributed to productive or counterproductive responses depending in large part upon capacity—that is, the conventional, social, personal, or professional resources available to staff (in part, the latter three mediated how and whether the first was used). There were gains as well as losses in the process. But when capacity was lacking or limited—by inherited conceptions of teaching or work norms, by too few opportunities to learn with knowledgeable others, or by prior knowledge and experience—then conflict was most often counterproductive.

When capacity was present—either through prior understanding; a sense of professional efficacy, experience, or belief (congruent with reform); through learning; or through social relationships created at the school—conflict could be a productive change mechanism or a stimulus for renewal and creative practice. That pattern held for individuals as well as for the organization or groups within it. For Mission Elementary staff, capacity meant much more than access to conventional resources.

Building capacity for ambitious reform at Mission Elementary was a complicated process that involved not only managing conflict—sometimes the process itself generated conflict—but at the same time transforming conventional "inputs" into productive professional resources. The staff's work at Mission shifts attention to a detailed perspective on what counts as "resources" for instructional improvement, and how such resources contribute to policy "enactment"—that is, how the agents and targets of very ambitious reforms make sense of policies and use (or do not use) the resources that accompany them.

Professional and Social Resources for Change

I use a broad conception of the term "resources" in this book, including what the individual educators brought to the task of reforming their curriculum and instruction: for example, their understanding, experience, sense of efficacy, and belief. Drawing on theoretical and empirical work, I treat personal and professional identities and interpersonal relationships as potential resources that can contribute to a school's capacity for improvement. Such a conception of resources allows for a more "elastic" view of capacity because it takes in what enactors are able to learn and the social capital or professional knowledge enactors are able to create from conventional resources—funding or materials, for example.

The story of Mission Elementary situates educators and their changing response to reform in the milieu of the district and the state, and the kinds of resources that they did and did not offer. The impact of the conventional resources that Mission's staff had available to them varied a good deal depending on how they used those resources—that is, how staff managed to use personal or professional strengths to transform traditional inputs into social resources or vice versa.

Thus, Mission's story draws on and deepens new conceptions of policy implementation, which have complicated traditional, instrumental views of the relationship between policy and practice (Cohen & Ball, 1990; Cohen & Barnes, 1993a; Cohen & Spillane, 1992; Elmore & McLaughlin, 1988; Fullan, 1993). At the same time, it builds on a more complex conception of educational productivity (Brophy & Good, 1986; Bryk, Lee, & Holland, 1993; Newmann & Wehlage, 1995; Purkey & Smith, 1985; Rowan, Guthrie, & Guthrie, 1986) than traditional input-output models. It illustrates how the term "resources" can mean more than the conventional, financial inputs to schooling. Rather, resources are also social, personal, and professional. Below, I elaborate on these categories.

In this book, the term "social resource" is informed in part by a "pedagogy of the policy" metaphor (Cohen & Barnes, 1993a, 1993b) which frames education policy "implementation" as the problem of engaging teachers (and administrators) in learning from and about the policy. Coleman's (1990) social capital theory also informs the idea that social resources reside in human relationships where there are shared goals, reciprocal understanding, trust, and so on. Thus, social resources might include, among other social relations, "scaffolding" for learning about reforms through sustained instructional discourse with knowledgeable others—"teachers" of the policy. Or, social resources might be mutually held goals for student learning, and collaborative conversations focused on how to achieve them (Peterson & Barnes, 1996).

These kinds of resources helped bolster capacity for reform at Mission, but they were modest when compared to the difficulty of the work. And, in the case of individual teachers, social resources for learning and change tended to be invented ad hoc, without official incentives, rather than available as an integral part of a district system. When the staff began to build capacity for change through mutual understanding and clearer goals, those social relations, while a potential resource for reform, also became a source of conflict. Social conflict was embedded in the social relations that had potential to build capacity for school-wide reform.

Like social resources, one aspect of the term "personal or professional resources" involves growth and learning, and is also informed in part by a "pedagogy of the policy" metaphor. Here again, I view "policy implementation" in part as the problem of engaging teachers (and administrators) in learning. From this view, the term "professional resources" is also a lens for considering the personal and professional identities that the agents of reform brought to the task of learning to enact them—that is, the prior understanding, experience, education, and predilection that enactors brought to their work.

Constructivist, cognitive theories of development—drawing from the work mentioned earlier by thinkers such as Piaget, Vygotsky, Dewey, and Bruner—hold that people interpret new information by building on existing cognitive structures. They interpret new information based on what they know and understand. The brief personal histories woven through each chapter in this book serve to illustrate a portion of what enactors brought to the task of interpreting the new information they encountered in reforms.

Using the pedagogy of the policy metaphor, one can imagine how the personal or professional histories of enactors inform our understanding of the "learners" of the reforms—the reform's end of the line, and likely most influential agents. At Mission, these personal and professional histories contributed to the set of factors in the school that sometimes complemented, sometimes competed with, but often complicated the reforms.

California, unlike many other states, had developed several elements of an instructional guidance system with the potential to help enactors learn from reform. Thus, continuing with the pedagogy of the policy metaphor, the CLAS was a potential reform "curriculum" for teachers, as were chunks of reform-oriented student curricula designated as "replacement units." The district and state curriculum frameworks served as a curriculum for teachers as well as administrators at Mission Elementary on some occasions. And the state school improvement process (SIP) that was centered on the task of aligning student work with the reform frameworks helped teachers at Mission specify the meaning of reforms for their particular classrooms.

Though holding great potential, generally, the elements of systemic reform, including those intended for instructional guidance, were set within a competition of priorities, conflicting messages from the state and the district, and "shopping mall" professional development norms. So, at Mission Elementary, these resources were thin when compared to the challenges of enacting the intellectually rigorous reforms. Recent budget cuts had further diminished their potential.

Coping with Conflict

While the staff at Mission Elementary responded ambitiously to reform ideas, conflicting purposes, conflicting commitments, and social conflict marked the process as they tried to make sense of those ideas. Adapting reforms to their situation entailed managing or coping with personal ambivalence, social clashes, and tensions in reforms—between competing ideals within the reforms as well as between the reforms and other notions of appropriate practice. Mission's staff also had to manage the tension between reform ideals and the practical realities in the school. How people managed in the face of those conflicts with only modest resources for the task at hand is the central theme that emerged from the study.

First, the curriculum reforms in their broadest sense—described earlier to include the ideals of staff collaboration, coherence, and rigorous intellectual achievement by all students—not only tended to compete with other programs or ideas about appropriate practice, but to compete (sometimes) with themselves as well. Further, the staff at Mission often seemed to embrace the competing goals. For example, aspects of curriculum reforms, in practice, tended to be in tension with some of the means and aims of the bilingual education program (either English as a Second Language instruction [ESL] or English proficiency). The reforms calling for high standards of intellectual achievement by all children interacted with bilingual education goals, which in turn seemed to be contradictory themselves at times. There were tensions within and between reform ideals in the case of Title I as well. The staff's choices around tensions—between the complexity in ambitious instructional reforms and the ideal of clear, specified goals, for example, or between commitments to both clarity and collaboration, for another—created trade-offs and losses as well as gains.

Second, aside from the problem of competing policy purposes, teachers disagreed with each other over what particular programs and policies meant and what to do about them (though until a significant decision to restructure the schools' work norms, such disagreements were not generally made public). And even when they did agree, they sometimes agreed for very different reasons. Teachers at Mission Elementary held conflicting beliefs about teaching and students, and those beliefs interacted with the meaning they made of various ideas.

Third, teachers and school leaders were ambivalent. Not only did they disagree with others about the meaning of policy ideas and what to do about them, but they disagreed with themselves about what to do. They were pulled in more than one direction at once. Finally, as noted at the onset, the policy and program ideals often were in conflict with the practical realities of life in this school as the staff at Mission worked to put those ideals into practice. A transient, poor, limited-English-speaking student population and dwindling resources are two examples of the "practical realities" this school, and many like it, face.

That conflict was part of the reform environment at Mission is not surprising: California was in political turmoil; the U.S. educational system is fragmented; the policy cycle is unstable. Personal, social, and intellectual conflict in the teaching and learning process, in schools or other such social organizations trying to change, have been widely reported (see e.g., Fullan, 1993; Lieberman, Wood, & Falk, 1994; Marris & Rein, 1982; Pechman & Feister, 1994; Purkey & Smith, 1985). But these accounts have generally not portrayed the need to manage conflict as an integral aspect of the reform process. Nor have they probed the issue of when conflict is productive or counterproductive for intellectually demanding reforms, and why. Finally, most accounts of conflict are not described from the multiple views of people working to enact ambitious reforms in schools.

In this book, the brief personal histories and interviews with teachers serve as one of several perspectives on the reforms and what it takes to enact them. While a staff's histories can contribute to a school's capacity for change, they are also a source of potential conflict. For all the commonalties in their roles and environment, educators are individuals. And, for the most part, in schools where autonomy is the reigning norm, personal histories, different sources of information and understanding, different educational backgrounds, and different convictions create differences in their practices. One assumption in the pedagogy for policy construct is that collaborative norms among educators have the potential to transform the differences in knowledge and understanding among teachers into sources of "scaffolding" for their learning. But these differences can also be a source of social conflict and disagreement, as they were at Mission Elementary.

OVERVIEW OF THE BOOK

This book grew out of observations and interviews I did with staff at Mission Elementary over a 2-year period. In all, I focused on eight people. (See Appendix for research procedures & data.) In the following chapters I have selected six of the eight people to highlight: A second-grade teacher, two third-grade teachers, a bilingual Title I teacher, a first-grade bilingual teacher, and the school's principal. Throughout the book, vignettes and interview text bring to life a version of what it would take to "leave no child behind" in American classrooms.

The book as a whole illustrates how the staff's collective choices around reform goals changed over time, and how such choices influenced the work of reform in classrooms. It begins in year one with a look at the Title I program, the bilingual program, and curriculum reform—school-wide and in classrooms—before a significant staff decision to restructure their improvement plan because of low test scores. Then the story line shifts to the school, classrooms, and to the small group of Title I students *after* some key events: for example, after the staff's decision to restructure and after the Title I bilingual teacher left the school. Using multiple views of the staff's response to reform ideals, of circumstances leading up to their decision to change, as well as those following it, I illustrate the conflict and capacity themes within and across Chapters 2 through 6.

Chapter 2 takes up those themes at the school level, by examining how competing policy or program goals and the principal's professional identity influenced school-wide renewal. In that chapter I focus the argument on the strengths and weaknesses of school-level reform in the first year of my research, and use the evidence to foreshadow the ironic twists the staff's collective response takes the following year.

The next two chapters illustrate variations on the conflict and capacity themes, focusing them more narrowly and deeply into classrooms, and the small group interactions between teachers and Title I students. Chapter 3 brings to life the realities of managing conflicting commitments in classrooms, and shows how two teachers' professional identities contribute to the school's instructional capacity. Those teachers—Anita Lorenz, a second-grade classroom teacher, and Monique Ponds, a bilingual Title I teacher—hold complex conceptions of teaching and student performances. This complexity subtheme becomes important again in Chapter 5, when it collides with the call for clear, common, school-wide goals and measures.

In Chapter 4, Lorenz's and Pond's small group of Title I students arrive in the third-grade classrooms of Kate Jones and Alice Michiels. Competing policy goals and very different professional identities create conflict between the two teachers. Their disagreements are a microcosm for some of the national, state, and historical arguments about educating American children. The chapter compares Jones's attitudes and mathematics instruction over time to illustrate how conflict may have contributed to capacity in her case. But the chapter also illustrates how their arguments undermined Michiels's capacity for improvement, along with her confidence in the reform practices she was just beginning to learn.

The next two chapters shift the analytic story line to the school, classrooms, and the Title I students *after* the staff began to implement their new, restructured, school improvement plan. In Chapter 5, the voices of key school leaders underscore the social conflict that emerged as the staff began to collaborate closely on clear goals: the more teachers clarified the meaning of their goals, the more they disagreed over what to do about them. At the same time, their work toward clarity tended to narrow the staff's conception of achievement. That worked against the complex conceptions of classroom instruction embedded in the curriculum reforms.

In Chapter 6 I focus on the tension that can occur between levels of activity: for example, between coherent school-level planning, and coherent instructional planning for students. Here I revisit the tensions among reform elements raised in Chapter 5, but elucidate them further through a closer look at Title I students' instruction in year 2. Contrasting images of that instruction after the new plan went into effect—in Juan Ramirez's, Alice Michiels's, and Kate Jones's classrooms—illustrate trade-offs for children and teachers. In this chapter especially, I attempt to show the nature of human resources gained and lost under Mission's new plan. In Chapter 7, the concluding chapter, I synthesize the book's macro and micro themes, identifying problems and suggesting possibilities for sustaining reform in American schools.

In this book, I examine policy implementation for its pedagogical potential with a primary focus on "the learners" of the policy—people in schools trying both to improve and maintain confidence in their professional practices. In spite of most policies' historically weak "pedagogy," I take understanding on the part of enactors to be one prerequisite for deep, far-reaching, and sustainable reform. In doing so, I have tried to develop an argument about the relationship between capacity building and conflict that should have relevance for how we manage complex social or individual change in education.

Like many similar schools, Mission constitutes the problems reformers want to solve, and the key agents for solving those problems. So-called high poverty schools such as Mission, schools that enroll many children who do not speak English, are becoming more common in the United States. In California approximately one out of every four children attending school lived in poverty in 1995. At the same time, one in four did not speak English (Education Week, 1997). And California, with 1.2 million limited English-speaking (LEP) students, was not even the state with the highest number: seven others had a larger number of LEP students. As the reform story unfolds in the chapters of this book, it shows that people in schools such as Mission Elementary will need to manage conflict, and at the same time transform conventional "inputs" into productive resources for improving instruction. Paradoxically, the capacity for doing such work is most likely to be lacking in those schools most in need of improvement. This view of the problem suggests several avenues for improving schools' response to reforms. But first, the story of Mission Elementary School.

CHAPTER 2

High Standards, Competing Priorities, and Complexity at Mission Elementary

The principal and teachers at Mission were coping with competing interests and limited resources for change in a school that compounded their challenges. They were working out the reform ideas in a school where many students were at risk for academic failure—either because of poverty or language barriers or both. Thus, in the first year of my research, before the federal standards reform initiative was in full swing, and before a significant staff decision to "restructure" their school mission, the leadership and staff were responding ambitiously to a difficult reform aimed at both reducing inequality and raising academic standards—that is, the California curriculum standards reform and Title I reform. But they were doing so in paradoxical circumstances that made their work extremely difficult. While the school's staff, students, and community were the reform's best hope for a successful enactment, they also embodied many of the problems that the reforms sought to address: academic, social, and language challenges is one example; contrary impulses toward multiple instructional goals is another; and inherited conceptions about professional norms, the principal's role, or school organization is yet another.

TITLE I AND CURRICULUM REFORM

During the 1993–1994 school year and for some time prior, at least a fraction of the teachers at Mission were responding to the state-wide curriculum reforms with some enthusiasm, adapting the ideas to their classrooms in varying degrees across several subjects—to some extent mathematics, to a greater extent science, and to a still greater degree language arts. Further, the Title I program in some respects resembled a model of the organizational reforms pressed in the 1988 Hawkins-Stafford amendments to the ESEA. Mission's staff had rejected "pull-outs" that focused on remedial instruction for Title I students, for example. They were using strategies that gave Title I students access to instruction which emphasized thinking and conversing about important subject matter content in "regular classroom" settings (Public Law 100-297). The staff at Mission were using categorical resources in ways that supported both curriculum and organizational reform.

This response to the first wave of reform was unusual for Mission Elementary. Laura Mather inherited the school when it was considered by some accounts to be the district's worst. She reported that Mission Elementary had been led by a series of rather passive principals, and most teachers there were not interested in innovation or reform. But Mather was determined to turn the school around and set out to do so. Over the past few years, she had been quite remarkable in her indefatigable campaign to improve Mission in the direction of equitable, high academic standards, to keep it running smoothly, and to create a nurturing community for the school's children.

She had hired staff who generally shared her belief in children, then worked to focus their commitment around it. She was able to do this in part because several teachers left when the former principal did. By 1993 when this story opens, Mather had hired 24 teachers, approximately four fifths of the faculty at Mission. Though she shared her authority for hiring personnel with a team of administrators and teachers, Mather had managed to hire some reform-minded teachers who seemed, for the most part, dedicated to Mission's students.

Mission's staff developed their Title I plan collaboratively and in conjunction with Mission's School Improvement Program (SIP). Louise James, the school's Title I coordinator, was also the School Improvement coordinator. She commented on those two planning processes: "We don't have a separate Chapter 1 Plan; it's all in the SIP [School Improvement Program] site plan." That sort of coordinated, school-level planning and coherent instruction for students, while allowed by the 1988 amendments to Title I, was about to be encouraged in the new Title I reforms—those initiated in the 1994 reauthorization.

Mission had not used "pull-outs" for their Title I students in 4 years—not since the 1988 amendments discouraged such arrangements. As Louise James put it in January 1993:

> Our Chapter 1 program is not a pull-out program. Many years ago it was. . . .
> But it didn't allow for children to be a part of what's going on in the regular
> scheme of things. . . . [Now] the focus is . . . to support these children during
> their regular curriculum and their regular instruction in the classroom, and so
> that's what we strive to do.

The instruction that most Title I students received in this school was generally integrated into regular classroom curriculum. Mather and James understood the plans to reauthorize Title I as confirming what they had been doing—that is, moving the program in the direction of high standards of academic achievement for *all* children. That was the direction in which the California frameworks and systemic reform efforts had been pressing. In the fall of 1993 Louise James explained:

> these ideas [in the proposal to reauthorize Title I] go right along with *It's Elementary!* and the direction of our state framework. For example, it says this is a proposal to "have the same high standards for all children . . . performance-based assessment, rich instruction, and support in the regular classroom, not a pull-out program". . . . For a lot of schools and a lot of places, that will be a big adjustment. But we've been working on that . . . here for a long time.

Thus, Title I instruction had been organized around the "regular curriculum" for some time. And, in this school, the regular curriculum was in the general direction of the standards-based reform ideas. James's reference to the California State Department of Education Elementary Grades Task Force Report, *It's Elementary!* (1992), and the frameworks is an example of the sort of standards she and Mather were trying to set in the school. A key recommendation of *It's Elementary!* is "Make a rich, meaning-centered, thinking curriculum the centerpiece of instruction for all students" (p. iii).

Mission Elementary's leadership and staff were generally committed to the curriculum reforms for *all* students. In language arts, children for whom one might hold low expectations were reading good books; speaking in public; writing stories, letters, and reports; taking part in interesting discussions. Many children who could not yet read were provided with one-on-one tutoring and conversation with thoughtful teachers or aides. These literacy tasks and practices are generally consistent with recommendations in the English-Language Arts Framework for California Public Schools (California State Department of Education, 1987a) and with the Model Curriculum Guide (California State Department of Education, 1988). In science, teachers at Mission were pressed to examine their students' work in that subject matter to reflect on how they were teaching in conjunction with the framework. The science framework asked that the students be workers—that they *do* science, not just read about it. It asked that their work not simply be activity, but also "minds-on" work, which leads to new understanding (California State Department of Education, 1992).

Finally, there were signs that teachers had at least accepted some of the big ideas in the mathematics reform and were trying them out. The proposed new mathematics curriculum adoption at the district level seemed aligned with the most recent framework ideas, and most teachers in this study reported liking the new program. With Laura Mather's and Louise James's support, some teachers at Mission were trying a few of the new ideas via "replacement units"—that is, special curriculum units designed in alignment with the reforms. They were attending workshops, consulting mathematics mentors, and so on.

Resources for Reform

Mission's staff and leadership used the conventional resources they had available—Title I funds, for example—to pay for professional development, to buy materials, to fund "extended year" or "extended day" Title I "academies," and to sponsor special parent nights. But they used most of the Title I funds at Mission to hire personnel. The staff shared in the decision to allocate these human resources—paraprofessionals and some special "hourly" Title I teachers—as equitably and evenly as possible, across all grade levels and classrooms. Thus allocated, resources were thin in many classrooms, and some teachers in the fourth and fifth grades reported that having one teacher for less than 3 hours a week didn't really provide the kind or amount of help they needed for their students.

"Teachers" and "Curricula" of Reform

Conventional resources aside, Mission Elementary was using the curriculum "replacement units," the Program Quality Review (PQR) process, and CLAS as resources for teaching and learning to build capacity for instructional improvement. Further, Mather was creating "social resources" for change by building a leadership team of like-minded teachers to help "teach" the reform to others. She generally delegated instructional leadership of reforms to lead teachers (in science and reading). This was especially so in the case of Louise James, who was quite knowledgeable about the Title I and language arts reforms, as well as a very trusted friend and assistant to Mather. A fifth-grade science teacher took the lead in a committee of teachers who were working on science reform. He also led the development of Mission's garden, which was used school-wide as part of an "integrated" curriculum for science, mathematics, and language arts. Finally, Laura Mather delegated some instructional and other duties to her vice principal.

This "leadership team" led the Program Quality Review (PQR), essentially an instructional process and resource for learning about science curriculum reform. The team, including the school's science mentor, created a professional discourse of sorts by collecting student work samples from all teachers, once each track cycle. The teachers selected these samples as "evidence . . . that students' work each year represents a well-balanced treatment of earth, life, and physical science in alignment with the district science matrix." "Essential questions" were given to the teachers in advance so they could think about their practice and about selecting work samples in light of the questions. During "walk arounds," the leadership team questioned students and talked with teachers.

The CLAS is another example of a resource for learning from reform—a potential "curriculum" for the reform, and one that Mission used. Mather, together with James and the vice principal, developed a "CLAS Action Plan" in order to focus teachers' attention on that assessment, and to help them understand what it expected of students. Mather sent James to an intensive 4-day training on scoring the reading and writing CLAS. James reported feeling "battle fatigued" when she returned, but nevertheless organized a "mini version" of the training she had received for teachers at Mission. She had them develop their own rubrics using samples of student responses they might categorize as better or worse than others.

The team of teachers and administrators Mather had put together was a social resource for the school; their relationship was a source of "social capital" supporting reform and Mather's leadership of the school. Mather trusted them and believed they were in agreement on a general vision for Mission Elementary.

From the view just sketched, it seems clear that Mission Elementary's leadership was committed to curriculum and Title I reforms. Mather, James, and others were responding to the call for high standards for all children much in the direction of the 1988 reform amendments. Further, Laura Mather and the school's instructional leadership supported the staff in their reform efforts and even provided some instructional guidance related to literacy and science reform. Finally, staff at Mission Elementary had developed a school mission together. And they often made decisions about resource allocation and organization collaboratively, generally spreading resources evenly, albeit thinly, across grades.

A COMPETITION OF IDEAS AND COMMITMENTS

But the principal and her leadership team were responding to the reforms in the midst of conflict: political controversy over goals, competing commitments, and competing ideas. So while the leadership and staff in this school were clearly committed to the organizational reform in the 1988 Title I amendments, and to focusing attention on the curriculum standards reforms, those weren't the only ideas in the air around Mission Elementary. In fact, the competition of ideas about educational aims and means was fierce in the MUSD and at Mission. For example, during this same year Mather was very concerned about Mission's low CTBS scores, and expressed uncertainty over what to do about them. Mather said:

> I think we are on the right road by looking at the bottom quartile. . . .
> What can we do for them? Unfortunately what we're finding is that . . .
> Even with [all we are doing for Title I children] it's really not enough.
> We still need to do something else. And I'm not sure that I know what
> that something else is.

But the CTBS and the CLAS expected quite different responses from administrators, teachers, and students. The CLAS tended to press for the effective use of language by students—varied, purposeful writing and student understanding of complex issues. The expectation here is for students to be disciplined workers—for example, that they think and actively construct their understanding of subject matter in the tradition of Dewey, Bruner, Piaget, and Vygotsky. But the CTBS tended to reward the rapid selection of answers to basic, more "factual" questions. Here, rote learning in the tradition of Thorndike is consistent. The CLAS assumed that a curriculum should be "meaning centered" and thus presupposed fewer topics, or big ideas, each to be considered in more depth for longer periods of time. But the CTBS assumed a more rapid coverage of a greater number of topics—not necessarily those in the state frameworks—in less depth. The CLAS asked students to think critically about the material they read, to look for evidence, justify their responses, and generally required quite complicated academic performances. The CTBS did not.

But for many people at Mission Elementary—especially the principal, her Title I assistant, and to some degree the staff—both of these tests seemed to represent "high stakes." And there is evidence from several studies that high-stakes tests can influence both teaching and the content of students' work (Madaus et al., cited in Darling-Hammond, 1992). These competing policy aims at Mission Elementary mirror some of the big social arguments about the goals of instruction in the United States.

Another example of competing commitments at Mission was in the pull between a child-centered "developmental" approach to educating children in the early grades, versus the idea of curriculum, grade-level standards. There were district committees and school-level committees with recommendations and possible courses of action for both of these reforms at Mission. Ruth Linn, one of Mission's teachers who sat on the district developmental education committee, expressed her concern over the fervor of district advocates and multiple reform strategies:

> It's almost like a religious experience for the people who created that
> [developmental] report card. . . . If you don't like the report card
> you're going to hell because you don't believe in . . . how they
> interpret the scripture. . . . It was a good thing to do. But like every-

thing else . . . it takes a lot [of effort]. . . . [Some teachers said] I'm really pressured this year and . . . this is just one more thing . . . I just can't do it.

Laura Mather talked about both standards-based curriculum reform and school renewal based on developmental education. She sent several teachers to a conference on developmentally appropriate instruction and others reported attending professional development activities focused on that idea. Classroom teachers talked about both. One teacher expressed confusion in a staff meeting over how to create a "non-graded" pilot that emphasized accepting individual differences in pace and content, and still hold high common standards for all children. She exclaimed: "Aren't we at odds with ourselves by trying to do both of these things?" They had been talking about subject matter standards, then switched to developmentally appropriate instruction.

So while the PQR process and the CLAS had the potential to be quite powerful curricula as well as guides for teaching and learning from the reforms, they were competing with other district and school priorities. Because of limited resources—time, personnel, and so on—that competition, as well as the large size of the school, diluted reform-oriented instructional guidance, especially when compared to the difficulty of the task of enacting reforms.

Generally, teacher predilection was the rationale for professional development activities. James explained how professional development funding from the SIP or Title I was allocated at Mission: "We keep teachers informed of the current [workshops] available and . . . if they see something they want to go to . . . they pull that brochure down and let me know." Teachers could choose from a range of options offered by the county, state, and district, which were posted in the lounge. While there were a number of content courses focused on curriculum reforms, there were also a good number that were unrelated to reforms and thus competed for the time and intellectual energy of teachers. Several of the latter focused instead on yet another of the MUSD's policy priorities—bilingual education.

The Confounding Factor of Bilingual Education

A large Spanish-speaking population and the multiple goals of the MUSD's bilingual education program complicated matters at Mission even further. Generally, the ideal of bilingual education, promoted by the MUSD, and to some extent by the California Department of Education (CDE), was based on three key goals: high curriculum standards, English proficiency, and integrated classrooms for promoting cross-cultural respect and understanding. Referring to California's *Bilingual Education Handbook* (California State Department of Education, 1990) and the bilingual compliance manual (California State

Department of Education, 1993), the MUSD bilingual coordinator reported the two "basics of any bilingual program" are English proficiency and rigorous content-based instruction in students' primary language. Such instruction should engage students in using "thinking, communication and problem-solving skills" (p. 17). Likewise the CDE pressed the goal of "cross-cultural" understanding. Mission's staff appeared committed to the three goals and made a creative attempt to address them.

But these goals, perhaps complementary in principle, tended to be in tension when the staff at Mission tried to put strategies into practice to meet them. For example, according to Mission's principal, several bilingual teachers, and some researchers, the first goal—high standards for all students—involved teaching students a core, reform-oriented curriculum in their primary language to develop both conceptual understanding and advanced thinking skills. Laura Mather explained her reasoning (and the district's) related to this goal:

> Well, as research says, [Spanish-speaking students] will learn in
> English as long as they have that conceptual foundation for language
> arts and math . . . in their primary language. Then they can learn . . .
> other subjects—science and social studies [and so on]—using lots of
> sheltered English techniques. . . . I think they learn [to speak] English
> by listening to English. [But] I do truly believe . . . that they [Spanish-
> speaking students] are going to be in much, much better shape to
> attain at higher levels in a second language [if they have a conceptual
> foundation in their own language].

In Mather's comments there are at least two important points that scholars of bilingualism have argued for some time: First, thinking skills acquired in one language transfer to a second language (Au, 1993; Hakuta, 1986). Second, making sense of academic content is a much different matter than simply listening or speaking informally in a second language (Cummins, 1982, 1989; Snow, 1992).

Thus, bilingual advocates argue, second-language students should be taught a challenging curriculum for conceptual understanding by methods that center on making sense of "rich content" in their primary language. They argue these kinds of "higher order" thinking skills are best learned in students' native language, then "transferred" to the second language. The principal, and many of the staff at Mission, referred to this research when they argued for such primary-language instruction and many seemed committed to teaching children a core curriculum for conceptual understanding in their native language.

But the second key goal of the bilingual ideal at Mission and the MUSD is to teach Spanish-speaking children to be English proficient. These two goals—

primary-language instruction and English proficiency—can be contradictory in practice, because when children are grouped by primary language in order to teach them subject matter for understanding—that is, the reform-oriented curriculum—they are not exposed to much English, thus perhaps frustrating the important goal of teaching them to be English proficient. Both Laura Mather and Ruth Linn, the bilingual mentor teacher at Mission, reported some parents' concern that their children were not learning enough English. And district policy as well as state law requires that students be taught to speak English.

Matters were complicated further by staff interpretations of civil rights laws, concerns about segregation, and cross-cultural respect—a third goal of the bilingual program at Mission. Staff, but especially Laura Mather, worried that grouping children by primary language amounts to a form of segregation. Several teachers, including Mather, reported that segregating children by ethnicity was unlawful as well as morally repugnant to them. Mather explained:

> it's . . . [a section of] Title Six of the Civil Rights Act. . . . Basically, you cannot segregate kids for more than [a certain] percentage of the day. I'm going to . . . integrate the kids more because . . . there's this class distinction thing that is occurring. There are the Anglo kids and there are "the other" kids. The "others" are Spanish-speaking kids. . . . It becomes a real problem.

Thus, grouping by language to teach for understanding can be in tension with other important goals of bilingual education in Mission Elementary—integration and cross-cultural respect and understanding. Early in 1994, Mather reported her "biggest" concern with Mission's bilingual program was that there "wasn't enough integration of Spanish speakers and English speakers." She was considering changing from primary language instruction to "mixed rosters" the following year—that is, putting Spanish speakers and English speakers together in bilingual rooms.

As a former bilingual teacher with a masters degree in bilingual-bicultural studies, Mather's interpretation of the multiple bilingual goals at Mission was complicated by her own quite nuanced understanding of the issues. Though she felt somewhat bound by the "late exit" district bilingual policy, Mather seemed ambivalent about it and about the findings from research that informed it. Citing both research and some of Mission's parents, she said: "It takes [students] 5 to 7 years to acquire the academic English, [but some students'] . . . parents, want them to learn . . . [English], sooner. They should have a right to do that I think." Here Mather's dilemma, informed by a mix of moral and practical concerns as well as by research knowledge, includes yet another question: not only is there the question of what to do, but when to do it.

Fragmented Days and Multiple Hats

In addition to managing tensions within the reform and its environment, inherited conceptions of principal's work, expectations from her district supervisors, and her own construction of the role combined to create a situation in which Mather spent much of her time coping with competing commitments. She has always given long hours to her school and at the time of this study continued to be involved in activities ranging from parent relations, funerals, fund-raising, and budgets to bus schedules, birthdays, and instructional reforms. Like many school leaders, she wore many hats, was subject to constant interruptions, and felt overloaded due to a long list of programs or directives from her school board, state, parents, and community groups (Fullan & Stiegelbauer, 1991; Greenfield, 1986; Peterson, 1986). Of her reform agenda, Mather quipped: "I have a list of about 16 major innovative kinds of things that we're supposed to be working on . . . just doing it as it happens. . . . Trying to stay one step ahead of the flu and everything else." Thus, like many principals, Mather was trying to manage competing priorities: The Title I and curriculum reforms—entangled with her bilingual education dilemma—were only two among many others.

Any given day might find Mather observing a teacher's instruction, in battle with district administrators over hiring practices, meeting with parents, or dispensing pencils—the last often in Spanish—to a small, dark-eyed child in honor of his birthday. One week she raised funds for a family so they could bury their child—one of her students—who had accidentally drowned. Another week she had to manage a community group who appeared at Mission— along with the local press—to plant the trees they had donated to the grounds. At the same time, a student from the next-door junior high school was reportedly armed and looking for one of Mission Elementary's staff because of an earlier altercation. Meanwhile a boy had wet his pants and was waiting for attention from the office staff. Another week obscene graffiti—again the work of neighboring junior high school students—had to be removed from the school. Mather supervised graffiti removal more than one early morning to be certain the school was clean when children arrived. Between scheduling transportation, looking at test results, studying dwindling budgets and spread sheets filled with the abstract representations of her diverse students, Laura Mather called these children in, one by one, to reprimand them for fighting. Then she talked to them about how they might learn to "get along," in the spirit of the school's conflict resolution project and her own aversion to conflict between ethnic groups.

The nature of Mather's work days at Mission Elementary is no exception to the general image constructed by researchers who have studied such work. Inherited conceptions of the principal's role press school leaders to be everything from administrator to lead instructor. As Cuban (1986) points out, there has long been a huge literature that calls for principals to "do it all." Mather's daily activities and comments are consistent with what Fullan and Stiegelbauer (1991) found in a survey of research on principals—that is, principals are torn in multiple, competing directions and generally feel overloaded. Fullan notes that principals are expected to be experts in at least six areas: school law, community relations, human resource development, student relations, administration, and instruction. Burlingame (1986) argued from results of a comparative field study of principals that potential school leaders should be "well versed in political theory" (p. 126) as well, because their "work structure" contains so many competing positions, values, and preferences. Dwyer (1986) and his colleagues found that among other work characteristics that successful principals possess (having a clear vision, for example), they also "stand at the vortex" of competing forces (p. 15) as they attempt to guide their organizations. Given the sketch of Mather's work and the inherited conceptions of such work, it is easy to see that curriculum and Title I reform were not only competing with other ideas about best practice, but the fraction of Mather's role devoted to acting as instructional leader of the reforms was also competing with other work priorities.

THE PRINCIPAL AND THE SCHOOL

Laura Mather's professional identity—including her experience, knowledge, and convictions—were a filter on the competing ideas and goals in and around Mission Elementary. Thus, the reform ideas at Mission (and the commitments Mather constructed around them) were charged with meaning that was deeply personal as well as richly historical—meaning informed by Mather's education, life, and the context in which she came of age in America. Mission Elementary's response to new ideas about curriculum and instruction was, to some degree, bound up with this principal—what she brought to the school and what she managed to learn about the reforms while on the job.

Professional Identity

At the time of my research Laura Mather was just over 50 years old, with short, brown hair; glasses; and a ready smile. She was divorced and had no children. Raised in the American West, Mather came of age in the 1960s, an era of social conflict and political polarization. She had earned a master's degree in bilingual-bicultural education, and had studied bicultural issues in Mexico under the auspices of the University of Arizona. Her education exposed her to considerable research evidence and theory related to native language instruction. But social action, especially on behalf of Chicanos, was also a central feature of her young adulthood. From an early age, the power of books and a passion for the equitable treatment of people have been important themes in her life.

As a child, after reading every book of interest in the children's section of her hometown library, Mather managed to get special permission to read from the adult section. She remembers the importance of books in her childhood: "The public library saved my life because . . . there was nothing I couldn't read [there]. I literally read the shelves."* Literature remained an important touchstone in this principal's adult life as well. She brought the personal and social resources for keeping her interest in literature vibrant to Mission Elementary—that is, regular conversations with a longtime friend and mentor about literature, theater, film, and so on.

In addition to the importance of literature, Mather's early experiences in the segregated Southwest, and her recollections of class identification, are antecedents to a principle she has tried to live by as an adult: that is, the ideal of equity among the many ethnic, racial,and economic cultures that make up the American heritage. That ideal informs the issues Mather systematically studied after graduating from college and upon which she reflects still—issues that by the 1970s had been labeled "multiculturalism." After repaying her college loans by working as a bilingual teacher in an impoverished New Mexico school district, Mather headed to a bicultural institute in Mexico, where she began a master's program in bicultural and bilingual education and became an activist on behalf of Chicanos. Importantly, the kind of traditional, disciplinary knowledge that the academic standards reform movement of the 1980s would draw upon was not a central concern when Mather and many others were educated for leadership in American schools.

Learning for Leadership

Thus, the formative themes in Mather's life—the importance of equity, a passion for literature, knowledge of her students' language and learning needs— gave her only part of the frame of reference she would need to lead the new, discipline-based reforms in the context of Mission Elementary. Further, Mather and her leadership team, though responding energetically to these reforms, were doing so with few resources for making sense of them on the job. First, the district's instructional guidance strategy was aimed at teachers, not at school administrators. Next, the district sent conflicting messages to schools

---

*This and all other quotations in this section were taken from interviews with Mather conducted in January and February 1994.

by pressuring school leaders to raise scores on two high-stakes tests. Viewed as "pedagogy," such messages created quite inconsistent, fragmented instruction about "the policy" and the meaning of reform for Laura Mather and others who were expected to lead reforms at their schools.

Finally, like most district administrators, those at the MUSD didn't construct their roles to include instruction. They never raised the idea that school leaders—as potential instructional leaders—would require opportunities to experience the kind of teaching and learning that reforms were pressing for students. So, for example, Mather met with other principals regularly under the auspices of her district supervisor's office. Those meetings might have been a source of learning, an instructional discourse for making sense of reforms. But a look at the agenda items suggests the discourse did not center on reformed teaching, student learning, or even changing school work norms. Rather, a long and wide-ranging list of items had to be covered. Occasionally reform was on that crowded list. Thus, while the monthly meetings were a potential resource for learning about curriculum reforms, they tended to also be a source of priorities or ideas that competed with reforms for principals' time.

Most of Mather's interactions with the district related to reform ideas—construed as "pedagogy"—might be characterized as inconsistent, contradictory, or didactic: District officials "transmitted" various policy messages to Laura Mather and Mission's staff, nearly in the form of mandates, often clustered with other priorities. According to Laura Mather, much of the professional development available to her from any source was not especially helpful. Nor was it pertinent to her learning needs related to curriculum and Title I reform. Mather cited the Association for Supervision and Curriculum Development (ASCD) annual conference as the exception to this rule. But her official opportunity to interact with this professional community was generally limited to once a year.

Despite Mather's weak, on-the-job learning opportunities, she had found and was using some sources for learning about the reforms—for example, she read widely about school improvement. But she was doing so without a "teacher" per se, without a clear or consistent "curriculum," without much time, and without much instructional or professional interaction with others.

Laura Mather's professional identity has no doubt been fostered by the particular places in West Texas where she attended school, came of age, left home, and attended college. Growing up and growing older, she has seen changing sensibilities around issues of race, language, poverty, and educational achievement. Brandishing a library card as a key to opportunity, and her personal standard of equity, by the first year of my research at Mission Elementary, Laura Mather had made a definite imprint on the school. That imprint was informed in part by the principle of equity and by her belief in the power of books for overcoming personal experience.

Capacity, Leadership, and the Status of School Reform

At this point in the story of Mission Elementary, Laura Mather and others were committed to curriculum and Title I reform. Mather had created "social capital" for the school by hiring like-minded, reform-minded teachers—Louise James, the vice principal, and others—then delegating instructional leadership to them. The leadership team generally agreed on Mather's vision for Mission, which included equitable academic standards for all children, and Mather trusted them to help her lead reform. In this sense, Mather was building capacity for change. She had created some of the individual and social resources the school needed. She also made use of some of the instructional resources her teachers needed to enact reform—the PQR process and the CLAS. So in some respects Mission did have a "curriculum" (the CLAS and frameworks), and the leaders who could serve as "teachers" of the policy to other teachers.

Moreover, drawing on the formative themes in her life, learning, and professional identity, Mather was, in some respects, reasonably well situated to move the curriculum-reform agenda in language arts forward: She had extensive knowledge of the students in her school—their culture, theory about how they learned, their language, and so on. She brought her passion for and considerable understanding of literature—including Spanish literature—with her to Mission Elementary, as well as a source for sustained learning in the form of her mentor and friend. Further, Mather had some experience in teaching adults, and was also quite an aggressive learner: She read widely, for the most part about topics she had learned about at conferences.

All of the personal and social resources for leading the reform, sketched above, likely account for some of the reformed practices in this school. For when ideas and precepts in the Title I and curriculum reforms are considered, in some ways this school was ahead of the federal curve. Before Goals 2000 and the reauthorization of Title I, Mission had embraced many of the principles contained in those reforms, many staff were trying to put them into practice, and from most reports instruction was less fragmented than it had been a few years before. Moreover, staff at Mission Elementary had developed a school mission together. Additionally, they often collaborated on decisions about resource allocation, generally spreading resources evenly, albeit thinly, across grades. Mather had encouraged the staff to plan together and collaborate on other matters as well.

But generally, that collaboration and shared leadership at Mission were filtered through inherited conceptions of school organization and autonomous work norms. For example, the staff at Mission was not collaborating on a clear, common, *school-wide* goal (something the Title I reform as it was tied to Goals 2000 would be pressing more vigorously by the end of this school year). As in most schools, teachers in this school had quite a bit of latitude to "do their own thing" (Cusik, 1983; Little, 1990; Lortie, 1975). An ambiguous school mission allowed a wide range of interpretations of the many program ideas in the school. One exception was the aforementioned PQR process, which did interject itself to some degree into teacher autonomy, as well as stimulate thinking and learning around a coherent vision of student work in science. But the staff, including leadership, appeared to treat the PQR process as one more project in a long list of projects that the school was undertaking.

Thus, while the PQR, the CLAS, and the curriculum frameworks provided instructional guidance for the reforms, they were only modest resources for learning at Mission, in part because they were competing with other priorities. Using limited professional development funds, teachers could choose from a large array of topics, some of which competed with the reforms. And teachers as well as administrators received "mixed messages" about what was important. For these reasons, reform-oriented resources for learning tended to be diluted. If professional development funds, staff energy, and leadership time had all been concentrated on the reform-oriented PQR and CLAS, then the "pedagogy" including the "curriculum" of the reform policy might have been a more powerful intervention.

The resource thinness was also due to the dwindling budgets, burgeoning student enrollments, and thus the lack of personnel in relation to the size of the school. Budgets at Mission had been steadily cut since Proposition 13 capped funding for education in California. Classroom size had grown: At Mission the average class size was 32 to 33 students, and modular aluminum classrooms were sprouting up around the school grounds. The instructional leadership team had multiple responsibilities, including classrooms of their own, and thus very limited time for instructional guidance.

Finally, inherited conceptions of the principal's role as well as the way Mather constructed it created competing priorities, thus diluting potential resources even further: Mather's time and expertise as an instructional leader, for example. A principal today is expected to fill a myriad of roles, ranging from budget analyst to instructional leader. Such superhuman performances are likely impossible just as implementing all the innovations that make their way into schools would be impossible. Nevertheless, when reforms are combined, even well synthesized or prioritized, they seem to assume school staffs will muster such superhuman capacity. So did Mather's supervisors. Her role was co-constructed based on inherited visions of leadership and it would have demanded considerable professional risk for Mather to reconstruct it without guidance and support.

In Laura Mather's case, education and background tended to complicate the manner in which she made sense of the reforms. Because of her continuing study of bilingual issues, and her sophisticated understanding of the research about how children learn in a second language, Mather embraced competing program ideals and found dilemmas where others might not see them—for example, the problem of teaching all children for conceptual understanding, teaching them English, and fostering an integrated learning environment. Finally, Mather's education did not provide her with the kind of disciplinary knowledge of subject matter that might have helped her lead curriculum reform (with the exception of language arts).

Thus, the prior understanding that she brought to the task of enacting curriculum reform for all students gave her only part of what she needed— especially when it came to the teaching and learning of mathematics. While Mather had personal and professional resources to sustain her interest and knowledge of literature and bilingual issues, she had no such resources in mathematics or science. Nor did she have any guidance or experience in leading organizational change (that she reported)—for example, managing conflict or reducing priorities. Nevertheless, Laura Mather was expected to lead mathematics, science, and organizational reform at Mission. In doing so, she not only had competing commitments and complex reforms vying for her time, but she had little in the way of "instruction" or a coherent "curriculum." Though the reforms required a great deal of professional learning, Mather had to be her own teacher.

Paradoxically, to create or use coherent learning opportunities, had they existed, she would have had to take the huge professional risk (for one assigned the task of "leading" reforms) of admitting she was a learner to her staff, her supervisors, and so on. To construct her role differently she would also have had to confront her supervisors at the district with the multiple competing demands they placed on her school—another professional risk. Or, in making her own and her staff's learning a priority, she would have had to ignore some of the many demands. For example, Mather might have learned from the science mentor at the school had she immersed herself in the PQR process. It would have taken a good deal of her time, but it likely would have also provided learning opportunities and professional discourse focused on science reform.

The sort of behavior sketched above demands a new conception of the role of principal as instructional leader—that is, the image of principal would include learning from classroom teachers in some circumstances, as well as from knowledgeable others—"teachers" of the reform. In this view, knowledge and expertise are distributed among multiple staff; knowledge is social in that leaders use what others know; and leaders learn from, as well as teach, others. But "leader as learner" is not something generally accepted in the inherited view of such work, just as "teacher as learner" is not part of the inherited view of teaching. The press for more "site-based management" in conjunction with new rigorous curriculum standards requires that both teachers and school leaders recast their roles. For professionals to admit to being serious learners is risky but crucial if reforms are to grow. Reformers should consider how to create "safe" contexts for such learning on the job, even as they are raising the standards for preparing a new generation of leaders.

CONCLUSION

A principal, unusual in her commitment and energy, had been working to create social resources and new professional knowledge at Mission Elementary by building a reform-minded leadership team who took joint responsibility for improving the school. The culture of both district and school encouraged innovation in instruction—that is, innovation in the direction of high, complex academic standards for all children. Title I instruction in the school was more rigorous and less fragmented than it had been before Mather's arrival.

But Mission's principal and her leadership team were responding to the curriculum reforms in the midst of competing ideas and commitments. The MUSD was pressing competing high-stakes tests—the CLAS and the CTBS—and potentially competing innovations—developmentally appropriate instruction and grade-based standards. Ambitious bilingual education goals sometimes competed with each other and with the reforms when Mission tried to put them into practice. Deep budget cuts exacerbated the repercussions of those competing priorities—one of which was to dilute resources for reform.

Capacity for change was further limited by inherited conceptions of schooling—organization, roles, and norms. For example, a laissez-faire culture (teachers often worked and learned quite independently) combined with mixed messages from the state and district to create some intellectual incoherence in the school. Mather had little time available for reflecting in a systematic manner on "the 16 innovative things" the school was undertaking, curriculum reform among them. Though Mission's leadership team was in many respects responding ambitiously to a very difficult reform, they were doing so by mixing the new ideas with traditional conceptions of school organizations—grafting old onto new rather than subtracting priorities or fundamentally transforming the school culture.

Moreover, the school's leadership had few if any powerful enough learning opportunities to transform inherited conceptions of leading, teaching, and learning. District administrators at the MUSD didn't construct their roles to include instruction, nor did they raise the idea that school leaders—as potential instructional leaders—would require opportunities to experience the kind of teaching and learning that reforms were pressing for students. Viewed as "pedagogy," conflicting messages from the district created quite inconsistent, fragmented instruction about "the policy" and the meaning of reform.

Mission's staff embodied many of the conflicting priorities in their environment. In this school, collaborative, democratic processes appeared to function smoothly for staff when competing ideals and their conflicting points of view about teaching or the meaning of policies were allowed to coexist behind closed doors and a hazy school mission. While there appeared to be collaborative decision making and consensus over goals at Mission Elementary, just behind their vague agreement and thinly allocated resources, conflict was brewing in the details. For good or ill, a momentous, "by consensus" decision to "restructure" their Title I curriculum would soon bring that conflict to the fore of staff interactions. I take up that decision and the ensuing conflict in Chapter 5. But first a look at classrooms.

CHAPTER 3

Managing Competing Commitments in Second-Grade Classrooms

Inventing a reform-oriented practice while coping with competing commitments and too few resources is not only extremely difficult, it is uncertain and demands complex judgments. Like many American teachers, Anita Lorenz and Monique Ponds were faced with challenges inherent in their practices: balancing competing ideas about instruction, for one; managing conflicting goals, for another. These tensions pose dilemmas that are endemic to the practice of teaching (Lampert, 1985; Lipsky, 1980; Lortie, 1975). But these two teachers were contending with competing interests in the context of a school that significantly compounded their challenges: they were trying to work out the ideas in the curriculum reforms with students considered at risk for academic failure because of poverty, language barriers, and other factors.

Just as important, Lorenz and Ponds were responding ambitiously to reforms with only modest resources for learning what the reforms required in the context of Mission. The curriculum reform lacked specificity or guidance for daily practice. While Mission offered more than many U.S. schools in the way of "curriculum and instruction" for the reforms, they were provided within a culture that did not constrain competing notions of best practice. Thus, learning opportunities focused specifically on the reform were thin. Nevertheless, these teachers managed to teach in the direction of the complex reforms due in large part to instructional capacity—capacity generated from the personal or professional resources they brought with them and the social resources they created while on the job.

CURRICULUM REFORM AND COMPLEX UNCERTAINTY

Anita Lorenz is one of the energetic, reform-minded teachers Laura Mather hired in her attempt to improve Mission Elementary. Lorenz was educated in the era of standards reforms and reported she "couldn't imagine teaching another way." By that she seemed to mean in a manner different from an integrated, whole-language approach, very much in the direction of California's language arts framework. She also reported using math journals, as well as teaching centers that focused on various strands of mathematics in the framework, including "logic and probability." According to Lorenz, her second-grade students were sorting, counting, and representing on graphs every manner of object and opinion in the room. These activities, too, were in the direction of the science and mathematics frameworks. It was clear during a year of observing her that Anita Lorenz held very high standards for all of her students.

But she also struggled with competing notions of what that might mean in a classroom of diverse learners. In essence, during the 1993–1994 school year, Lorenz was inventing a challenging instructional program, trying to manage the tensions between the sometimes opposing ideas in light of her students' needs: She struggled to balance a reformed whole language curriculum—that is, notions about interactive learning, authentic language use, and "higher order" thinking skills—with ideas about direct instruction of basic word attack skills. And she worked at balancing her belief in high common standards with her belief in individual learning "modalities" complicated by the range of students in her classroom. These are not easy tasks and they required complex, informed judgments rooted in Lorenz's knowledge of her individual students, the subject matter, pedagogy, and learning. Balancing competing commitments required that she manage in the face of dilemmas (Lampert) and make difficult decisions often in the action of her classroom.

Curriculum Reform

Given a panoramic view of Anita Lorenz's room, a visitor would first be struck by the sea of small faces—from pale to deepest shades of brown—topped by hair ranging from straight blond to curly black. Her classroom was a microcosm of California's cultural and linguistic diversity. Next, Lorenz would come into focus. Young and attractive, with dark eyes and long, black hair, Anita Lorenz was often a blur of motion in her room. I saw her sitting at her desk only once and that is when the children were out. But she often came to rest somewhere in the classroom by one or more students, most often crouched by them in conversation, eye to eye.

Generally, Lorenz's language arts practice included a reform-oriented core curriculum of authentic language approaches for all of her 32 students: She expected them to read the same literature, complete the same writing assignments, and take part in the same literacy community within her classroom. All of the children in Lorenz's room read, wrote, or were read to every day. Anita Lorenz reported she believed in the writing process, and she used writers workshop strategies—instruction very much in the direction of curriculum reform in this state at the time. The children and teacher spoke easily of their writing and the various "stages" it was in: a first draft, an edited copy, and so on. At the end of the 1992–1993 school year, she explained how all students could participate in writing:

> The thing that's nice about writers workshop is . . . it accommodates everyone's level [of development]. . . . Children who are at the picture-book stage—[I] work with them to expand ideas. I might choose the word "balloon" and have them write the letter B at the top. So you're encouraging as much writing as [any] child can handle. Or they might tell you . . . "we're going to the store and we're going to a party." [You respond,] "Well, I see that you're in the car and I see the store, but I don't see anything about a party." . . . [And,] "Why are you going to the store before you're going to the party?" [They respond,] "We're buying a cake."

In this excerpt, Lorenz explains that "writing" in her classroom means communicating effectively and expanding ideas for all her students, even if a student is learning sound symbol correspondence at the same time. Here, as well as in many other examples, Lorenz pushes *all* of her students to think—about connections between story details, about reasons for actions, about being precise—no matter where they may be starting from, in their writing or reading.

Often, Lorenz used cooperative learning groups, another feature of the curriculum reforms. Children sat in groups of four and were encouraged to talk as well as help each other with their reading and writing. They told stories while others wrote them down; they wrote stories using invented spelling or even letter sounds, as in the excerpt above; they illustrated stories and "read" them to others. Lorenz reported often she had "kids read other children's work and edit for one another." But according to Lorenz, this sort of collaborative work did not come automatically to her students:

> Kids aren't going to be comfortable helping each other unless it's required and you teach them how to do it. . . . I give them a lot of assignments that would be impossible to do unless they help each other. Once they're used to that, then I think they freely begin to help each other whenever they need it. . . . They know that they're allowed to talk and get help as long as their talking is about [schoolwork] and it's quiet.

Observations confirmed Lorenz's explanations of her instruction and classroom work, here and further above. Her students worked together on factual reports, creative stories, reading books, and other projects. They talked frequently and quietly about their work. When she wasn't leading whole group

activities—"group writes," for example—Lorenz was walking around the
room, stopping at various groups of four to observe, question, or help. Her
classroom walls were covered with samples of the students' writing and the
writing of others; and there were tables, shelves, and cupboards filled with
good children's books.

The California language arts curriculum guide argues that teachers should
elicit and use students' experiences or "prior knowledge" in instruction.
During class discussions, Lorenz often appeared to do just that: she asked
questions that drew on what her students might already know or feel—their
"prior experience." These questions were open-ended; her students responded
with their opinions and she encouraged multiple responses. In the brief excerpt below, Lorenz explained that she wanted the children to have thought
about a story's themes before they read it, and to have connected it to their
own feelings and thoughts.

> *Lorenz:* L, how would you feel if you really thought everyone forgot
>   your birthday?
> *L:* Mmmmm. Sad.
> *Lorenz:* Sad. How would you feel Ch?
> *Ch:* Mad.
> *Lorenz:* Mad! L would feel sad and kind of down. And Ch would be
>   mad! (Here she evoked an angry tone) "You know, they forgot my
>   birthday. I can not believe . . ."
> At this point one little girl interrupted to exclaim, "How rude!" And,
> Lorenz picked up the beat with, "How rude!" Several others mumbled,
> "How rude!" and the children began chattering about the awful
> possibility of people forgetting their birthdays. Lorenz interrupted
> their chatter by asking Ch how she would feel.
> *Ch:* I'd feel sad [and something not audible] then I'd throw my own
>   party.
>
> (Field note, 2/8/94)

Here, Lorenz's practice is in the direction of curriculum reform and reflects
cognitive learning theories which argue that students should learn to use
the strategies that successful readers use—strategies such as "activating . . .
background knowledge" (Palincsar & Brown, 1989). The excerpt is also an
example of Lorenz using her students' ideas as a source of information and
knowledge for the group. Lorenz explains: "I like the children to hear . . .
what the [other children] think . . . it gives them a wider range of ideas
[about] how a person could even feel on this day." Here she wants to challenge her students to move beyond their own experience, to consider the
merits of multiple opinions.

But not just any opinion will do in Lorenz's class. For example, at one point in her language arts lesson, Lorenz said to the entire group nestled around her near the front of the room, "Can you think about what [the story] might be about?" When a couple of children gave answers that didn't seem to meet her standards, she pushed for more details, "try to be more specific" and "two people have given really good specific examples. Can you think of a specific example?" In yet another example, a little girl responded, "Valentine's Day" to Lorenz's question, "What does this month make you think of?" Lorenz queried her further: "Why did you think that?" The girl explained she had been thinking of love and friendship, and Lorenz asked, "Now what do you think birthdays and love and friendship have to do with one another?"

In the first exchange Lorenz pressed students to be clearer in their thinking, to provide more concrete details so others might better understand them. In the latter example (as well as many others) she pushed the student to provide reasons for her response and to make some connections between her thinking and the theme of the discussion. In these examples, she also pushed some students to think aloud so that others might use their reasoning as "scaffolding" to become more skilled "thinkers" themselves (Resnick & Klopfer, 1989). Generally, Lorenz's practice as sketched above is in the direction of curriculum reform that called for students not only to read important literature and use language with fluency, but to be critical thinkers when they read, talk, and listen. Consistent with a reform rooted in cognitive theory and in a disciplined conception of literacy, this teacher's instruction pressed students to use language and the thinking of others to find meaning, but also to communicate effectively with others.

A Competition of Ideas: Phonics and Basic Skills

Clearly, literacy and curriculum reform ideas could be found in room 201 at Mission Elementary. But Lorenz had not adopted the reforms wholesale. Notions about phonics, basic skills, and direct instruction were also sprinkled throughout her teaching practice. Teaching children to look for patterns as a tool to help them read and spell was an idea vital to her instructional repertoire:

> There are some basic rules. In general for the level our kids are writing, if there is a silent "e" at the end, the vowel is going to be long. . . . Why not teach that idea to them so that when they go to spell, they can sound out words a little bit better and spell them a little bit better?

At the beginning of the 1993–1994 school year, Anita Lorenz had been slowly revising her practice to incorporate more skill instruction—she called this aspect of her practice a "whole-language spelling program"—and said the reason for her change was that her students "need it." She reported that during her first year of teaching in Los Angeles, all her spelling words came from the literature she used to teach reading—this was consistent with curriculum reform ideas she was learning about in her methods courses—but, no longer. Because "by the end of the year I didn't feel it was very effective. If they were good spellers already they left being good spellers. And if they were poor spellers they left being poor spellers."

For 2 years Anita Lorenz had been thinking about how to develop a program that used literature and "whole language" approaches, but which included some discrete basic skills and spelling tools—that is, phonics as well. She worried aloud about getting the "right balance." One of the tenets of the reform is that students should write for authentic and varied audiences. On some occasions she tried to make phonics "authentic" by creating an "audience" for worksheets. On other occasions she managed to stretch simple vocabulary lessons into group conversations with the goal of "making sense." Lorenz adjusted her practice based on what she believed her children needed, what she believed "worked" in her classroom, and on competing ideas over how best to educate "disadvantaged" children.

Lorenz was working in the territory between two big ideas about teaching and learning, long debated among educators, and she was managing in the face of competing commitments. One was her commitment to creating authentic literacy activities for all her students; another was her commitment to seeing that all her students write and read aloud according to standard English conventions by the time they left her classroom. She seemed loathe to dismiss the former for children who were struggling and would likely be judged by their ability to do the latter. In Lorenz's case, the conflict theme begins to take shape in her ambivalence and uncertainty over competing instructional ideas.

Common Standards and Individual Differences

For Anita Lorenz, the demands of inventing a practice were complicated by the range of differences in her students' ability to do the academic work she required of them. Lorenz worked hard at creating an environment that challenged all her students. But in doing so she had to adapt her rigorous core literacy curriculum to the individual differences in her students. She reported being helped in this endeavor by her conviction that children have different strengths, weaknesses, and different learning "modalities." These convictions Lorenz held as strongly as those about core curricula, phonics, and new ways of teaching literacy. Here is a teacher trying to respond seriously to multiple aspects of the standards reform—both curriculum reform and Title I reform—

and because of the context in which she is working, the complications of her job have multiplied.

Through a monumental effort, and the help of one, part-time paid aide, Lorenz created an ambitious Title I program in her second-grade classroom. She considered the program part of her "developmentally appropriate" core curriculum, which to her meant "You're dealing with kids no matter where they are. . . . It's adapt[ing] your curriculum so that you meet the needs of all your kids." For Lorenz, "adapting the curriculum" to meet her Title I students' individual needs did not mean lowering standards. As noted earlier, while she respected each of her students' strengths, she did so with one eye on where she wanted all of her students to be. She pushed her Title I students to think, even if it meant, in some cases, expanding a sentence by one or two descriptive words:

> Something as simple as a word, getting them to expand the idea of the word, will . . . prepare them that much more for . . . expand[ing] the idea in a story. . . . "I saw a big ball." Well, what color was the ball? "Brown." Well, how big was it? "Very big."

Lorenz's expectations were demanding, no matter where a student was beginning. And her Title I students often seemed to rise to those demands: They pushed themselves.

She reported often having four or more activities going on simultaneously. Her report was evident in her practice. While some children sat in clusters of three or four reading silently, a few were grouped around Mary Johns, the Title I aide, and Lorenz. These children read aloud, haltingly, and were helped by the two adults. Still others were seated at a small table with headphones over their ears listening to Lorenz read—on tape—the same story that many of her students read silently to themselves. Still other children might be sitting knee to knee in what Lorenz called a "triad read-around"—a heterogeneous group reading to one another and helping one another with words.

Through these methods and more, *all* of Lorenz's students had access to the "same" curriculum. But for some of her students, "reading" meant "listening" to the story at a "listening center" or in a small group of children reading orally. All the children were "writing" stories and informational reports, usually in cooperative groups. But for some students "writing" meant "telling" stories to an adult who would write key words from the oral account on the child's journal paper, then ask her to fill in the story with invented spelling. Or, writing meant illustrating a story through pictures. Or, Lorenz would write stories on the chalkboard in whole-group sessions, encouraging all students to contribute.

To adapt her core curriculum in this way, Anita Lorenz made good use of her Title I aide's time—an hour and a half 4 days a week—in relation to the reforms. She sought and won Title I funds to pay for release time in order to teach her aide the ways of Writers Workshop, and how to question children to draw out or expand their ideas. But she reported needing more help to do her job the way she thought it should be done, and she feared losing what she had: "I need more hourly help. . . . I need more support. . . . I need that person [Title I aide] here [more often] . . . if I lose my aide I don't know what I'll do." At this point in the story, Title I resources were allocated thinly, but quite equitably, across all grade levels school-wide. Further, Mather and James reported the "greatest need" was in the Spanish-speaking rooms where Chapter 1 children were concentrated. Lorenz was teaching mostly English-speaking children, so she didn't receive the Title I bilingual teacher's help.

Thus, Lorenz told me, it was her innovative classroom management, her one, very valued Title I aide, and her volunteer recruitment that made it possible for her to do her job the way she felt she should. To manage her resource problem, and to help her create the literacy environment she wanted, Lorenz spent a good deal of time and energy recruiting junior high school students, parents, and a grandparent, as well as teaching her own students how to help each other. On any given day an observer would find extra instructors in Lorenz's classroom—ranging in age from very young to old—working with the students. Lorenz reported using tutors and parents to help her keep students "on task." Tutors helped children with their homework in the afternoons while others were working independently, and after school. She told me that just having parents in the room improved her students' performance. Research confirms her report: Parent involvement is considered one key aspect of programs that are successful in educating "disadvantaged" children.

To this observer, Lorenz seemed to be managing more than one classroom on any given day with a dizzying array of organizational and instructional methods. A single young woman, Lorenz reported expending most of her time and energy on her teaching. She mobilized the resources she needed to respond to individual students in a meaningful way, while pushing them all toward high standards. Lorenz put forth an Herculean effort to do so, and she expected similar effort from students.

A Closer Look at Two Title I Students

A close-up view of Gerard and Kyle, two of the Title I children who have struggled the most, according to Lorenz, shows how she managed to adapt her core curriculum to individual Title I students and how she measured progress toward high standards in her classroom. These children also demonstrate what it takes to achieve those standards, and the arguments Lorenz had with herself even as she maintained them. Lorenz was conflicted over just what to do. But one aspect of her instruction was constant; it cut through the many seemingly contrary notions Lorenz held: This teacher had high expectations for her students. Her expectations appeared to place enormous demands on her personal life and the lives of her students. These children and this teacher provide an image to keep in mind when considering "what it will take" to achieve the high performance standards for all children set out by curriculum and Title I reforms.

Lorenz assigned homework every day. She went to great lengths to see that it was returned by each child the next morning. During one of my visits, she actually had some problems with parents because she was demanding so much from their kids. The vice principal was getting complaints. Lorenz responded that she "knew" these students could do the work; they just had to put their minds to it. She thought they would fall "farther behind" if they didn't do the extra work.

During this same visit, she told me about one of her students, Gerard, who despite difficult circumstances—he lived with several siblings and parents in very close quarters—always returned his homework on time. She told me that Gerard never complained about his homework. And she felt his family members were supportive, but probably didn't have the time to help him much (though she required that all parents help their children with homework at least one night a week and asked them to "sign" their children's work).

When Gerard first joined Lorenz's class, he could only read a word or two and he could not write. Lorenz talked about her efforts to get him started:

> It took him a half hour just to get his name and date on the paper. . . .
> I would have to go over five and six times in a thirty-minute [period],
> every five minutes, to get him back on task. I might get two letters of
> whatever we were doing before I came back and got two more letters.
> I'd say, Gerard, just write this word.

But Lorenz saw strengths in Gerard: "Every now and then he would say something that was so insightful and so mature in thought that . . . he perplexed me." What did it take to see Gerard make progress? How did Lorenz adapt the curriculum reforms to meet his needs? What were Gerard's needs?

As noted earlier, Lorenz believed an integrated language arts program— reading, writing, listening, and speaking—was important for all her students, but she also believed one of Gerard's special strengths was listening: "His modality is auditory learning." Lorenz explained further:

> Gerard . . . he's amazing! . . . I swear if I sat him down with a tape
> recorder . . . he would shut that thing off and tell me what they said.

And he would remember the vocabulary. He's in RSP [resource specialist program], but as far as his auditory learning ability, he's just brilliant. . . . [When] I question the kids . . . his hand shoots up and he remembers the most minute details. And he also gets the main idea.

Thus, Lorenz tried to address Gerard's individual needs throughout the year, but she never abandoned her goal to have him read aloud and write sentences (even though, according to her, writing was not his strength). How did she do it?

Gerard, along with another child, Kyle, are two of the children who worked with junior high school tutors on their phonics homework assignments, and with the Title I aide "telling" their stories. They also sat at the "listening center" during silent reading time. There they listened to a variety of tapes on all manner of subjects, from social studies to science. Then they would join the class discussions, often making interesting contributions, according to Lorenz. They both attended Mission's Title I "academy." The academy was a program that extended the year for Title I students to provide them with additional instruction during their intercession. By the end of the year they were both making some progress. While Gerard began the year pulled out for special education, by midyear he was remaining with the group. He could read and write a few sentences and even read in front of the entire class on a couple of occasions. Lorenz reported: "He's really made a huge amount of progress. . . . He still gets behind, but . . . he endures."

But during one visit near the end of the year, Lorenz also confided her ambivalence about the work she had accomplished with Gerard. "Maybe I'm expecting too much from second graders," she thought out loud one day. She had discovered that Gerard was spending hours every night at home on the assignments she was giving him. She had not known he was working such long hours. She felt badly about pushing him so hard and told his mother, "If he spends more than an hour on homework, don't let him do it anymore! . . . I want him to play. He needs to play . . . he works too hard." Lorenz was uncertain about her standards. She compromised by having junior high school tutors help Gerard with his homework assignments at school. The rest he continued to finish at home.

Like Gerard, Kyle could read and write by the end of the year as well. But he began the year sitting with his head down during language arts, according to Lorenz. Sometimes he would cry or put his hands over his face. Both Lorenz and her Title I aide were worried about him. He was so discouraged. But near midyear, he suddenly began to write a bit, then read aloud; and he became, in Lorenz's words, "so excited" for having done so. The following excerpt from a writers' workshop lesson captures the exchange between Kyle, Lorenz, and the Title I aide, the day he began to write:

Lorenz said, "All right, tell me about your picture." Kyle said something very softly and Lorenz said, "Who are your friends?"

Kyle responded and Lorenz said, "Okay, you had friends."

Kyle interjected something and Lorenz said, "Oh, you called them on the telephone! Okay, you called your friends on the telephone and what are you up to?" (Kyle explains something.) Lorenz said: "Oh, so you're sitting on the couch, calling your friends, telling them it's your birthday!" (All this time she was writing some of Kyle's words on his journal paper with a fine-tipped magic marker.) Kyle had a grin on his face as he explained his picture to Lorenz. She was crouched down, eye to eye with him, and was also smiling. She continued to repeat/paraphrase the story Kyle was telling her. Then Lorenz said, "Okay, let's see if you can read your words." She put the journal paper down on the table and pointed to the first one. Kyle stared silently at the words.

Lorenz: It is your what?

Kyle: Birthday

Lorenz: And you are . . . ? (pause) You called your . . . ?

Kyle: Friends

Lorenz: Good! You're sitting on the . . . ?

Kyle: Couch

Later, Mary Johns [the Title I aide] turned to Kyle and asked him what sentence he would use for "friends." Kyle decided "my friends are coming." Mary nodded approval and Kyle went back to printing. When he finished, he had written the following on his journal paper: It is mi birthday. my friends are coming.

(Field note, 2/8/94)

Here is an example of writing as "telling" and another instance of Lorenz's adaptation of language arts reform. Through dictation—something the language arts curriculum guide suggests teachers use—Kyle is able to do the same writing assignment as his classmates in preparation for reading and discussing the story about a forgotten birthday. Kyle's curriculum is the same as that of his classmates, but the method is different.

There were curriculum standards in room 201 at Mission Elementary. Lorenz set them and she and her aide monitored the progress of the Title I children toward them. Though Lorenz "adapted" the core curriculum to meet Gerard and Kyle's needs, she always pushed toward another horizon: "You have . . . to make them want to write and keep pushing them to be better, more accomplished writers." Later the same day, Lorenz said to her aide Mary Johns, "Kyle is finally starting to write!" In the midst of the chaos around them, while children were running about preparing for recess, Lorenz and Mary looked at each other and smiled at this recent development: Kyle was start-ing to write. At the end of the 1993–1994 school year, Lorenz and her Title I aide counted Gerard and Kyle among their victories, even though some of the second-grade students were writing, "marvelous [two-page] stories."

Anita Lorenz's effort to teach literacy in the general direction of the cur-riculum and Title I reforms shows not only the difficulty, but the *complexity* of an ambitious response to these reforms: It is filled with competing ideas, conflicts of conviction, and uncertainty over both. There is the complexity of sorting through and managing a flurry of sometimes competing instructional ideas—for example, she wondered if she was including enough basic skills work in her instruction, or too much. A myriad of ideas had arrived there at Mission Elementary, from multiple sources, such as conferences, Lorenz's education, workshops, and policy documents. The culture of the school and district at this point in the story did little to prioritize or diminish the compe-tition of ideas in the school, no doubt increasing the uncertainty of respond-ing to reforms.

There is also Lorenz's uncertainty about her instruction in the face of com-peting commitments: for example, in the midst of pushing her students to improve academically, she wondered if she was pressing too hard. She re-ported the need to nurture her young charges as well as push them. Further, in honoring a commitment to one important ideal in the reform, she had to respond to "the prior knowledge" of a tremendous range of students. In hon-oring another important reform principle, she had to compare them all to rigorous academic standards. Lorenz was constructing a practice that main-tained two important, though potentially contradictory, ideals of the curricu-lum reforms in dynamic balance.

THE POLICY AND PRACTICE MEET
IN A TEACHER'S PROFESSIONAL LEARNING

One way to account for Lorenz's ability to manage an ambitious response to reform while coping with conflict is to consider her teacher education. That education was unusual because the ideas in the two big reform themes sketched in Chapter 1—academic standards and new conceptions about learning—played an important role not only in what Lorenz believed about teaching, but in how she learned it.

Anita Lorenz had been teaching for about 5 years when this study began in the spring of 1993—a fact that surprised her a great deal. After graduating in 1988 from a California university with a degree in art, she began working for the design department of a southern California business. Lorenz soon dis-covered she was unhappy with such work. On advice from a friend, the following fall she took a teaching job in the Los Angeles area using the "emergency credential" California initiated in an attempt to remedy the teacher shortage there. For the next 3 years she taught each day, and went to her college methods courses each evening.

When recalling the impact of her life experiences on her current teaching practice, Lorenz repeatedly referred to three components of her teacher education program that were especially important to her learning: first, the regular discussions she had with her mentors, professors, and peers; second, she often referred to the curriculum materials organized around the California curriculum frameworks; and third, Lorenz talked about the authentic nature of her coursework which, in addition to the focus on subject matter frameworks, was also embedded in her novice classroom practice.

Anita Lorenz reported that having two experienced, practicing teachers and one university professor watching her instruction, then providing her with ongoing feedback, was extremely helpful in learning to teach. These people visited her classroom regularly and she talked to them often. Furthermore, she reported having regular discussions with her fellow students and with university professors who were teaching the methods courses. They also talked often about teaching and curriculum, both inside and outside of class.

Lorenz described an educative process in which shared norms included both challenge to novice teachers' assumptions—critique and debate—as well as support for trying out new ideas or working through problems. Instructors built on students' "prior knowledge" when introducing new information—for instance, "they helped you come up with ideas to build on what you were doing." Further, the learners in Lorenz's community were not simply receiving instructions about how to teach; they were treated as a source of information and knowledge for the group—as "scaffolding" in cognitive learning terms. Finally, in the teacher education process Lorenz described, the curriculum was rooted in part in the students' own problems of practice.

Not only was Anita Lorenz able to learn about teaching through challenging discussions rooted in her own experience with classroom problems, she was also able to build on what she understood using some of the big ideas in California's curriculum frameworks—one of the key instruments of curriculum reform in that state. For example, in mathematics: "My math teacher . . . really focused on the framework. She taught us the different strands of mathematics, and our unit had to include 14 math lessons—two for each of the strands." Lorenz reported having courses like this one in language arts, and social science as well—courses where she was required to develop curriculum units based on different elements in the frameworks.

In all her talk about coursework, Lorenz often emphasized the pragmatic, purposeful nature of her teacher education around the state frameworks: "The assignments that we did we were using. We didn't create a [curriculum] unit that wasn't going to work in our classroom. . . . People were excited. . . . We had a lot of questions because we were [working in classrooms every day]." Both her assignments and questions were authentic because they were centered on her practice. Here, Lorenz's "active engagement" in the subject matter appears to have been a source of internal motivation.

Lorenz described what theorists, cognitive psychologists, and social scientists from John Dewey and Jerome Bruner to Belenky, Clinchy, Goldberger, and Tarule (1986) have argued about learning: Important understanding grows out of purposeful, intellectually challenging activity—that is, when learners wrestle with and bring knowledge to bear on important problems in interaction with others. Most of the important characteristics of the education Lorenz described were unusual for university classrooms (Goodlad, Soder, & Sirotnik, 1990). But then, as outlined in Chapter 1, the currents of thought about teaching and learning that were gaining prominence in California in the 1980s were also unique in recent history, and Anita Lorenz was there.

Thus, not only were the twin themes of the reform ethos—disciplined academic standards and cognitive learning theory—in her practice at Mission Elementary, but the learning community Lorenz was creating in her classroom, permeated with social constructivist assumptions, was in many ways similar to the one in which she had learned to teach. Further, Lorenz seems to have emerged from her program willing to question her practice and embrace complex problems. Whether her toleration for complexity and uncertainty can be explained through learning opportunities or personal propensity (likely both play a role), the habits and attitudes Anita Lorenz emerged from her program embracing are nonetheless unusual.

Armed with her prior experience of learning while practicing within a professional community, Lorenz also created some social and intellectual support for herself while teaching at Mission: She made a point of conversing with colleagues and even visiting and observing classrooms when she was "off-track." She sometimes talked to colleagues very directly about teaching goals. For example, she reported telling a first-grade teacher: "I'd like to see you make it a goal that all your children can write a complete sentence when they come into my class at the beginning of the year." After some conversation, the first-grade teacher agreed to try. Thus, in this instance, the two teachers were beginning to forge mutual goals: Lorenz could craft her expectations to build on what her students knew or could do after first grade. Lorenz did not want to be isolated in her teaching: "My . . . expectations [are] . . . to team with the other grade levels and the other people in my [grade-level unit]. . . . I do not wish [to be] isolated. I want to work in a team." Lorenz's behavior and attitude in seeking out interdependent relations with teachers at Mission Elementary was unusual—not just at Mission, but unusual for American teachers generally.

On a related issue, Lorenz was quite serious about thinking of herself as a learner. She often reported seeking out colleagues in order to learn from them. For example, she said of another teacher at Mission: "We're going to mentor each other." She spent time observing classrooms in order to learn from other teachers. And, early in the study, when asked about the meaning of often-used terms such as "developmentally appropriate instruction," she responded: "I'm still at the stage of . . . trying to learn what that means." Lorenz seemed comfortable admitting she was a learner, and she sought out opportunities to learn from varied sources: her colleagues, her students, conferences, and college coursework.

It is not surprising that Lorenz was also attending to the reform-oriented "curriculum and instruction" that Mission Elementary School offered through the PQR process. Lorenz reported that process had prompted her to begin "taped assessments" and graphing projects to develop samples of her students' "understandings." She used the tapes in her teaching and in discussion with the leadership team. And, Lorenz's students were collecting and sorting objects by color and size, then making graphs representing what they found. She was "thinking about trying three variables—color, size, and shape." The PQR was a social resource for Lorenz's learning, one that stimulated reflection on her practice. But just as important, Anita Lorenz was able to effectively use the school PQR process as a resource, in part because of the professional resources she brought with her to Mission Elementary.

While Anita Lorenz was unusual in her habits of seeking out colleagues and learning opportunities, still she was working in a culture typical in American education, where her choices for learning could be idiosyncratic. The district and county offices offered extensive learning options focused on everything from Egyptian art to ESL and "Self Esteem in the Bilingual Classroom." A pamphlet listing the courses opened with this: "The workshops listed in this book reflect the survey of teachers' interest and priorities." Teacher preferences in this district ranged far and wide.

UNCERTAIN JUDGMENTS AND PRACTICAL CONSTRAINTS

The curriculum and Title I reforms intersected with the bilingual education program though the Compañero project—a team of teachers collaborating to coordinate instructional goals in English-speaking and Spanish-speaking classrooms. During the 1993–1994 school year, across the verandah-like hallway from Anita Lorenz's room, a small group of Spanish-speaking, second-grade children worked with their bilingual Title I teacher, Monique Ponds. Ponds's small group is another view into Mission's adaptation of curriculum and Title I reform *before* the staff decision to restructure them. She worked an hour each day for Ruth Linn—Lorenz's Spanish-speaking counterpart—helping Spanish-speaking Title I students learn the "regular curriculum."

Like Anita Lorenz, Monique Ponds was adapting a version of the curriculum reforms—an integrated language curriculum, only in Spanish—in ways that made it more accessible to her charges. And they, too, were making some slow progress, according to their teacher. But Ponds was also similar to Lorenz in that she was ambivalent about her practice, uncertain about sometimes contradictory commitments. Further, practical concerns were sometimes in conflict with the program principles of Reading Recovery—a key element of her Title I instructional program. For example, the central tenet of one-on-one tutoring conflicted with a combination of limited funding and a great number of students in need.

Ponds tried to organize her work with students in the direction of Title I reforms. Though she pulled her students aside to work at a small table, in order to provide them with more "motivation and support" than they would receive in the large group, she stressed that the Title I program was not a "pull-out"—an organizational arrangement the Title I reforms had discouraged. She reasoned that the small group work was coordinated with the regular curriculum. And Ponds reported that within the safety of a small, close-knit group, she was able to motivate her students toward more challenging academic tasks than she might have without it.

Ponds talked about her students' needs: "Most important is motivation. More than anything else—motivation and support." She explained that the Title I students are just arriving in this country "and they're scared to death . . . not catching on." Ponds used three of her small charges to illustrate her point. For example, she stated, "[Maria is] capable, but needs organization, motivation. Nan? I'm sure she doesn't get a lot of support at home. A lot of the students are just immature." Yet another very small girl, Ana, "was born out in the bush in Mexico, very premature . . . they set her up in a little shoe box and put lights around her." Ponds's observations about the instructional needs of Nan, Ana, and Maria—the young Spanish-speaking girls she tutored—were evident in her small group interactions with them, as described in the following field note:

> During a lesson in which members of the small group were writing a short report on what they "wanted to be," Ana, an especially tiny girl with a deep brown complexion and long hair, began sobbing because her eraser had torn her paper. The group seemed to take her outburst in stride and offered her immediate support: Nan, a talkative girl with a long braid hanging down her back, got up casually, walked over to get a tissue, then silently wiped the tears from Ana's face. She left the

tissue with Ana, who began twisting it, seemingly still agitated. Her lip was still quivering and she continued to twist the tissue in her hand.

Ponds began taping the torn paper and said in Spanish, "It's okay, Ana. You can write here on the side, or with another sheet. Or I can write something for you on the other sheet so that it doesn't take so long."

In all, the ministering took only moments, and Ana soon set back to work, finishing her report but only with continued urging from Ponds. When she finished, she read it, albeit haltingly, to her teachers.

(Observation note and Recording, 5/94)

In this group, adapting the curriculum to the needs of individual children consisted in part of creating a nurturing environment in which children could then be pressed harder to think, write, and read than might be possible in a large group.

Ponds's instructional goals—motivation and support—are another instance of a teacher pulled in more than one direction at once. She tried to maintain a balance between what could be thought of as contraries: pressing or "motivating" her students toward the hard work of academic achievement, while nurturing or "supporting" her small charges who, new to this country and school, were "scared to death." She did this in part by teaching the children in their native language.

Ponds's quest to balance nurture with the kind of pressure that would motivate these children to work hard toward difficult academic standards is not as simple as it might seem. Nor is Anita Lorenz's work of maintaining similar commitments. Curriculum standards competed with other urgent concerns for the time and energy of Mission's students and teachers. Like Laura Mather, and most teachers in this study, Ponds talked frequently about the lives of her students: One girl's father tried to hang himself after a history of violent abuse. Another boy's mother was in jail; yet another boy's grandmother had passed away, leaving the child suicidal because she had been his sole emotional support in a rough life. The problems some children faced in just living, let alone learning, made pushing them toward the hard work entailed in the policy visions even more difficult for Ponds and Lorenz.

This type of competition between a program ideal and practical considerations illustrates a key difference between Monique Ponds's and Lorenz's versions of Title I: The former teacher is an enthusiastic novice in a program grounded in considerable research evidence—Reading Recovery—which gives her some warrant for her practices (Pinnell, 1990). But even armed with technical knowledge and research-based authority, and though she worked with a smaller number of students, Ponds was still uncertain about her practices, for she was constrained in what she did by her circumstances. Ponds reported her approach to teaching the bilingual Title I students was "a very modified" version of the Reading Recovery techniques because of two reasons: first, she was in a high turnover position and there weren't any funds to send her to the yearlong training; second, the materials and methods were all prepared in English, not Spanish. She coped with the conflict between the program ideal and her practical constraints by adopting some of the Reading Recovery methods, rejecting others, and translating the materials—forging her own version of the program.

On the one hand Ponds may have frustrated important aspects of the Reading Recovery method through her creative compromise. On the other hand, without Ponds's personal effort to translate and to learn this aspect of the program, her students likely would not be exposed to some of the instructional techniques that reformers and researchers say help children learn to read. The clash between program tenets and the lack of resources created a dilemma for Ponds. Her adaptation of Reading Recovery precepts was how she managed.

CREATING INSTRUCTIONAL CAPACITY
FOR COPING WITH COMPLEXITY

Despite differences in their situation and practices, both Monique Ponds and Anita Lorenz were managing to teach in the direction of Title I and curriculum reform. The important features their reformed practices had in common here are *conflict, complexity,* and *uncertainty*: These teachers were coping with conflict—between practical constraints and reform ideals, or between competing commitments—and in doing so they made complex, uncertain judgments. Their practices reflect considerable ambivalence and a willingness to hold contradictory ideas. Further, these two teachers' inventions were not supported by a "hard ground" of technical knowledge or public agreement, even in the case of Reading Recovery, which Ponds had to adjust considerably within the context of Mission.

One way to account for the similarities in the way they managed the reform in the midst of conflicting messages and practical constraints is to compare their teacher education programs and other opportunities they had for learning. The educational opportunities Ponds identifies as most important to her practice were similar to Anita Lorenz's, and in part, those opportunities were linked to instructional leadership at Mission Elementary. An attractive young woman in her 20s with dark hair falling over her shoulders, Ponds had worked at Mission as a Title I bilingual teacher since May 1992. But even before then, she worked as an aide there while getting a Liberal Arts degree in Bilingual, Bicultural Studies with an emphasis in Spanish from a local college and state university. Monique Ponds was part of the Bilingual Teacher Corps, a group of student teachers who spent a year working in schools funded by a federal grant. This is when she became acquainted with people at Mission Elementary. So, like Anita Lorenz, Ponds had been in an intern program, and worked in classrooms while attending methods courses.

Also like Lorenz, Ponds had several "mentors" who were practicing in the direction of the curriculum reforms, and she studied the curriculum frameworks with college professors during her coursework. Two of Ponds's "mentors" were teachers at Mission Elementary. Ponds spoke highly of several staff there and said they had always treated her as a "teacher in process." But she was especially attached to Alice Michiels, the third-grade bilingual teacher.

Ponds also talked about the guidance she was receiving from Louise James—one of the school's key instructional leaders and the Title I Coordinator. In this instance, with Laura Mather's support, James and Ponds invented a resource for teaching and learning, though there were few incentives in the system for them to do so. James had a link to instructors outside of Mission Elementary because she was engaged in a yearlong study of theory and practice related to Reading Recovery funded with Title I money. She helped Ponds learn the basic tenets of that reform-oriented program. Monique Ponds, like Anita Lorenz, was curious and eager to learn, and she had read all she could on the subject of Reading Recovery methods. But James was a valuable instructional resource for Ponds.

Ponds and James spent time observing one another, and James acted as an instructional guide. The two teachers carried on a professional discourse of sorts, albeit limited by time constraints. James observed Ponds and provided helpful comments after the lessons. Conversely, Ponds observed James "model" Reading Recovery lessons and they talked quite often about books related to Reading Recovery. Both James and Ponds were very quick to say what Ponds did was *not* officially Reading Recovery. That qualification would come only with more education, time, materials, and money. Ponds said, "In the meantime, I just hope to attend some in-services and soak up whatever I can from Louise." Ponds counts this opportunity to learn, along with her intern program, among those experiences that have influenced her practice quite significantly.

CONCLUSION

Despite coping with competing commitments and practical conflicts, Lorenz and Ponds responded ambitiously to both the curriculum and Title I reforms. Both teachers managed to teach in the direction of the complex reforms in part because of personal and professional resources they brought to the job—for example, a general disposition toward using enormous reserves of effort and energy. They used their personal resources to build more instructional capacity. Lorenz sought out extra human resources she needed for her classroom. Both Lorenz and Ponds were aggressive at creating or taking opportunities to learn about teaching whenever they could. They both seemed to think of themselves as "learners" or "teachers in progress." They sought out colleagues and conversed with them about their teaching. Though there were few system incentives for doing so, they invented ad hoc structures for learning on the job. Essentially, both Anita Lorenz and Monique Ponds managed to create social and intellectual support for their learning and their practice in the direction of reforms. That behavior on their part is unusual because norms of "privacy" or "autonomy" generally still persist in schools.

Moreover, both Anita Lorenz and Monique Ponds were educated during an era of reform. These teachers—both relatively new to teaching—brought ideas about reformed teaching with them to Mission Elementary. They both described their teacher education programs as providing opportunities to learn from curriculum reform (instantiated in the California frameworks and worked out in classrooms while they were interns). They both reported having mentors during their teacher education with whom they spent considerable time talking about reforms. By her reports, Anita Lorenz was taught in a manner similar to the way she was teaching when this study opened.

Finally, Lorenz and Ponds managed to teach in the direction of reforms in part because the ideas they brought to the school were reinforced in the MUSD and at Mission: The district and school supported their efforts to some extent. The school leadership certainly didn't oppose the reforms, and they offered a few resources in support of learning about them. The MUSD curriculum guide is consistent with the state frameworks, for example. The PQR process at Mission, as well as the CLAS, served as a "curriculum of the policy." Instructional guidance was built into both of those. Such pedagogical policy mechanisms were unusual and more ambitious implementation strategies than many states employed at the time of this study.

In responding to reform, both teachers were coping with complexity: They made difficult, uncertain judgments in the midst of practical constraints and competing conceptions of best practice. For example, innovations in the direction of integrated language use, critical thinking, and conversation are not necessarily conducive to improving standardized test results (Darling-Hammond, 1992). But such results were a goal for Title I students in both the scenarios outlined in this chapter. Thus, reform ideas competed with traditional goals, especially for disadvantaged children. Ponds and Lorenz were also committed to supporting their small charges while at the same time pressuring them toward high, grade-level academic standards. Despite differences in their particular situations, maintaining these sometimes contradictory commitments was part of their daily work.

Both Ponds and Lorenz were also managing with what they considered to be too few resources to do the job the way they wanted. So, for example, Ponds's adaptation of Reading Recovery was a compromise, based on her situation: too many students, too few funds for training. Her invention for learning Reading Recovery with James was a response to the dilemma she and the school leadership faced in finding themselves with children who badly needed help, but without the resources—trained personnel—to serve them. Likewise, Anita Lorenz was unable to manage her reform-oriented classroom without recruiting many more human resources than Title I funds provided. She was aggressive about doing so, but she was also unusual.

Here an important point to note is that the complex nature of these teachers' adaptations in the midst of dilemmas does not lend itself easily to technical rationality. One example of such rationality called for in the Title I reform is "coherent" school and district-level planning, including "clear, common goals" and "accountability for results." Another example often used as a strategy to implement reform policies is training teachers to replicate practices. Related to the former point, the teachers' instructional choices in this case make sense in the context of their classrooms—they are even ambitious responses to reform ideas—but they are not necessarily conducive to goal clarity and results aggregated at the school and district level. Rather, their practices are based on uncertain judgments rooted in part in their particular students, and their understanding of teaching and curriculum. What they expect from their students is also not easily reduced or represented in the aggregate.

Furthermore, practical circumstances (lack of time, money, language barriers, and so on) often thwarted reproducing the program ideal, even when their practices were based on more specified methods—methods more conducive to coherent school-wide planning or "teacher training," as in the case of Ponds's Reading Recovery adaptation. Her example highlights the problem of assuming a technical or coherent "transfer" of reform ideals through "training." In these classroom images of curriculum and Title I reform, the uncertainty and complexity of practices that are in the direction of "high standards" are not necessarily, but can be, at odds with the ideal of coherent school and district-level planning based on aggregate accountability measures or common practices. In this case, as the story unfolds in Chapter 5, it seems that the two ideals were at odds with each other.

CHAPTER 4

Conflict and Change in Third-Grade Classrooms

The interplay of conflict and capacity continued in year 2 of the study—the 1994–1995 school year. That year, when the two small groups of Title I students left second grade, most of them went to the third grade Compañero team of Kate Jones and Alice Michiels. These two teachers, as with many others at Mission, disagreed about methods and goals, sometimes quite passionately. Though the staff had made a school-wide decision to work more collaboratively on a more focused school goal at the end of the past school year, most of the leadership's effort was directed toward the lower grades—kindergarten through second. Thus, before and even after the school-wide decision to work toward common instructional goals, Jones and Michiels disagreed about teaching, what their students needed, and what various policy ideas meant for their practices. Their differences interacted with the competing policy assumptions in the CTBS and the CLAS. Personal and professional identities and competing policy ideals created a good deal of conflict during the 2 years the teachers worked together.

While the many conflicts of conviction between Jones and Michiels seemed to heighten uncertainty for Michiels, who was trying very hard to change her mathematics practice, such conflicts, by repeatedly challenging deeply held assumptions, appeared to have opened Jones to change, to the possibility of learning about reformed practices. Here again—as in the internal conflict so prevalent in the complex inventions of Lorenz and Ponds, for example—the theme of coping with conflict was intertwined in the daily work of adapting policy ideas to classroom practice with only modest resources to support that process.

AMBIVALENCE: AFTER THE CONVERSION, THEN WHAT?

Alice Michiels, like Monique Ponds and Anita Lorenz, was ambivalent about much that she practiced. But this was especially so in her mathematics teaching, which she was working hard to change, in part because she was trying to make difficult transformations in circumstances that made that work even harder. First, unlike Lorenz or Ponds, she had to unlearn much of what she had learned in her teacher education program. Next, she was doing this work in the midst of conflict—a competition of ideas in the district and school as well as daily disagreements with her partner. That situation seemed to heighten her ambivalence. Finally, Michiels did not have enough of the resources she needed to support her changing mathematics practice.

In the early 1990s two events reportedly changed Alice Michiels's way of thinking a great deal: She got married and she first heard about the mathematics framework strands. With regard to the latter, she credits the local county math mentor (who, according to Michiels, was trained by Marilyn Burns) with "shocking" her into trying to change her mathematics teaching:

> I realized, oh my God! I've been teaching this old-fashioned way. I never knew there was another way. That's the only thing I'd ever learned, the traditional way—you teach algorithms. . . . In my eyes, I just changed overnight. . . . She [the county mathematics instructor] had an extensive background in math. I just couldn't believe it. I was shocked.

She admitted in the 1994 school year that she was still struggling with that change. It had not been easy for her. She said: "You change little by little. You can't just jump over to a new way of teaching. I tried to do that and almost killed myself." She continued:

> I was stressed out because I couldn't do it all . . . they told you here are all the strands. Well, you can't possibly . . . know how to do all the replacement units unless you go to the training. So I've been going to the training and learning the different ways. [But] you still have to keep some things intact while you're working on learning how to teach the new way.

One important point in Alice Michiels's comments here and further above is that she had to unlearn as well as relearn central aspects of her instruction while retaining sole responsibility for her classroom. In this instance, her ambivalence was related not simply to competing commitments, but to change and loss—a letting go of some portion of her former expert identity. Coping with the uncertainty inherent in teaching becomes much more difficult when a teacher is casting aside some portion of her professional self, becoming a novice after years of teaching in order to transform her practice. The uncertainty between the "old" reliable construction of meaning and the "new" or untried can be extremely threatening (Heaton & Lampert, 1993). It can produce discomfort akin to grieving (Marris, 1974). When change involves loss—even when such change is desired—the "disorientation" can be a source of "profound anxiety" (p. 149).

The process of enacting mathematics reforms did seem especially difficult on a very personal as well as professional level for Michiels. Her response to curriculum reform in mathematics appeared to cause her a good deal of emotional pain. Her discomfort was apparent in her earlier comments —"I was stressed out" and "[the change] almost killed me," for example. Further, at one point she confided her belief that she had hurt her past students by teaching them to do algorithms by rote methods instead of teaching them to understand mathematical concepts. Michiels worried that perhaps she had "reinforced their misconceptions," as the woman teaching her about the reforms explained she might.

Another important point here is that Michiels did not have the benefit of learning about these reforms in the context of an ongoing support group of peers and instructors as did Lorenz (and to some extent Ponds and Juan Ramirez). While the curriculum reforms had *challenged* Michiels's assumptions, she had little *support* for changing her practice. In Michiels's case, support was especially crucial because her reservations and uncertainty about the reforms were not so much a matter of will as of capacity. Michiels had embraced the curriculum reforms with a fervor that marked many of her life's choices. But she felt quite unable to do what the reforms required in the domain of mathematics, and she had to learn in the midst of her daily teaching, with only modest resources to support her changing practice.

According to Nemser (cited in Elmore & McLaughlin, 1988), surviving the uncertainty of change requires feedback from knowledgeable others, time for reflection, and interaction with colleagues. "Mastery" requires "safe rehearsal opportunities" among other learning opportunities, and time for that rehearsal in the company of trusted others (pp. 45–46). Rand researchers have also reported that in addition to "pressure," teachers need "support" for successful change, including opportunities for constant interaction among staff, and access to knowledgeable mentors who can respond to concrete classroom problems (McLaughlin, 1976, 1987). Such resources include a "teacher" of the reform, materials, or a curriculum, as well as a professional community— for trying out new practices, for having them challenged, for revising them and trying again.

But neither Laura Mather nor Louise James had the expertise or the learning opportunities themselves to prepare them for the role of instructional leader in the domain of mathematics. And although the school culture was changing, those changes did not yet provide Michiels with the collegial support and interaction that could have bolstered her reform attempts. Thus, various workshops and the support of her principal—both financial and moral—seemed to be enough to persuade Michiels to change, but they were not enough to support or sustain the learning that such change requires.

Coping with conflict with too few resources appeared to heighten Michiels's ambivalence and may have been counterproductive to the reforms' progress in this instance. During the 1994–1995 school year, Michiels seemed adrift, somewhere "between math facts and math concepts," because when she stopped teaching students the facts completely, shortly after her change in beliefs, she noticed "they never did [learn them]." Her internal conflict was exacerbated in part by her *Compañera*,* Kate Jones. She spoke with some disdain about aspects of Jones's style, but then said: "Her CTBS scores are the best." At least four other people at Mission Elementary offered that same information, unsolicited. By all reports, Jones's students scored well on standardized tests. Thus, while the school had responded ambitiously to the curriculum reforms, those reforms were still competing with other goals and methods, even after the all-staff decision to forge a clear, shared sense of purpose.

A CLASH OF ASSUMPTIONS

The case of Alice Michiels and Kate Jones shows two teachers whose beliefs clashed over everything from teaching and students to what policy ideas mean and what to do about them. Many of their disagreements mirror the long-standing debate in this country over the aims and means represented by CTBS and by the CLAS—a debate going back at least to E. L. Thorndike and John Dewey. When the small group of Title I children I observed in Anita Lorenz's room left second grade, those who spoke English went to Kate Jones's third-grade classroom. While Jones and Lorenz both talked about classroom management—rules, discipline, and the like—their students' swift transition between blocks of work time was the only way in which their classroom organization was similar. Students moving from Lorenz's reform-oriented classroom to Jones's classroom experienced very different instructional environments across grade levels.

But these students had to adjust within grade levels as well, when they traveled back and forth between Michiels's and Jones's classrooms. Jones was by some accounts quite a drill-oriented teacher. By all accounts, she was the most traditional teacher in the subset of teachers I observed at Mission Elementary, and she had resisted the curriculum reforms more than any other. Thus, when Michiels was struggling with new ways to teach mathematics, the no-

---

Author's note: Compañera, the feminine form of *compañero,* means "friend" or "companion" in Spanish.

nonsense Kate Jones was simply rejecting the new ideas. That had changed by the end of the study, but not before the two decided to part ways after teaming in the Compañero project for 2 years. Kate Jones was skeptical about many of the reform ideas that Alice Michiels was using. "Where in the real world would a child find unifix cubes?" she wondered.

While Michiels was experimenting with math journals, discussion, and trying to learn from her students' thinking, Kate Jones was complaining that Michiels's students did not know their "facts." Consistent with Jones's belief that discipline is a key to good teaching, Jones's students knew their multiplication facts better than any others: She drilled them on those facts and others nearly every day. Michiels talked about her differences with Jones in this way:

> I'm struggling with [my mathematics teaching] because my partner is using the more traditional approach. I'm listening to what she's saying. She doesn't do the [framework] strands at all. She doesn't believe in manipulatives. . . . We're like day and night. But she does an effective job with them [students]. I don't know. What do you do? Her kids know the facts better than anyone but she drills them into them. I don't know. I think they will pick it up when they're ready. But . . . I've also found that by not [working on the facts] they . . . never did [learn them]. So I'm kind of . . . in between, kind of in between.

Not only do we hear Alice Michiels's ambivalence here, but it seems that this ambivalence is bound up in part in her conflicts and disagreements with Kate Jones. Differences of opinion and practice have the potential to be a resource for learning and scaffolding for teachers, as they were, for example, in the education of Anita Lorenz. But here such disagreements were not conducive to creating a "safe" context in which Alice Michiels could "rehearse" her new practices. In this school and district, where ideas about best practice competed, conflict between teachers made Michiels's reform work riskier than it might have been in a context where teachers school-wide agreed on reform goals. Such agreement would have been a value added social resource for Michiels.

Michiels and Jones also disagreed on most other matters of practice. For example, Michiels has been steeped in the theory and practice of bilingual education and second language learning. She seemed to believe quite strongly that teachers had to connect school knowledge to the cultural knowledge that students brought to school. Michiels had a passion for understanding other cultures in order to make these connections for her students. At the beginning of their partnership, Kate Jones really didn't understand what "all the fuss was about." She reported that students—all students—could learn "the basics" through self-discipline and practice. (Michiels later changed Jones's mind about this matter, a bit.)

Though Jones had adopted some of the literacy reforms—a version of the writing process, a writing portfolio, required core literature, and so on— her instruction still featured the "basics" that she believed benefited all students—phonics, for example:

> I [always go] back to phonics-based [instruction] because I find children—if they can't sound out words; they can't spell; they can't read. . . . The more I work with children, the more I see a need for getting back to basics.

Phonics was central to her literacy program for all her students and, unlike Michiels, Ponds, or Lorenz, Jones did not work to integrate phonics instruction into her reading and writing lessons. Jones used phonics and spelling much more traditionally as separate elements of language arts. Again, Jones's views were rewarded by her students' achievement. In spelling bees, Jones's students sometimes won even when competing with older students in higher grades—a fact of which Jones seemed quite proud and brought up often. She talked about cooperative learning:

> Children learn from children . . . [as much as] they do from teachers. They have to rely on their neighbor. You'd be surprised how they help each other . . . I believe in the team concept . . . even though my classroom isn't set up in the groups of four that most people consider cooperative learning.

Nevertheless, she most often encouraged competition, or seemed ambivalent about student collaboration versus student competition. In addition to the spelling bees, Jones's children have competed against the upper grades on "math facts." Jones explained:

> They learn them by rote . . . beginning with [multiplication and going to] long division, which is all the book takes it to . . . you need to reinforce goals . . . through repetition. You're gonna get better the more you practice, it is my theory. My children will walk out of my class [knowing their math facts]. . . . Last year my third graders beat the fourth graders in multiplication facts. I . . . found a fourth-grade teacher . . . and I said, I'll take your kids on.

In these comments, we can hear Jones's penchant for competition and following the textbook, as well as her tendency toward drill and practice methods—all traditional approaches to teaching mathematics.

While Jones relied on rules and especially competition to motivate her students, Alice Michiels (like Lorenz and Ponds) tried to create "authentic" reasons for students to read and write in order to "motivate" them. In contrast to Jones, Michiels tried to avoid drilling students and spoke with disdain about that method, even as she seemed to ruminate over the observation that her students "didn't know their facts." She responded to Jones with pride in her own students' achievement. They could understand what "the facts" meant:

> My kids may not have memorized stuff like some of her kids have, but they probably can tell you *why*. I'm going to put this problem on the board five times six—tell me three ways that you can illustrate that? And they will, you know, they'll say okay that's five groups of six or that's five circles with six stars in them each.

Michiels sometimes encouraged multiple answers (though did not seem to be deft at doing so), and she tried to encourage cooperation among her students. To that end she allowed lots of conversation and chatter in her classroom. Jones allowed practically no talking at all, even in her "cooperative learning groups." Michiels's transitions from one lesson to another took a long, long time. Jones's took less than 60 seconds; she set a timer and her students hustled. Michiels's students also hustled when they were in Jones's classroom for "mixed groups." Jones's room was organized in a traditional manner: Rows of desks faced the front, toward the teacher. Michiels organized her students in small groups facing one another, in order to foster group work and conversation.

There were lots of other striking contrasts between Jones and Michiels, and these *compañeras* appeared to have had a rough year working together. The students had to make adjustments as they traveled back and forth between the rooms: To talk or not to talk, that was only one of the questions for these third graders. Michiels and Jones opted to split up their partnership at the end of this school year. But in the fall they were having a debate in their classrooms that was in part a reflection of the larger, longer-running debate about education in this country and in California.

The disagreements between these two went deeper than the competition of ideas in the school, state, and country over how to best educate America's students. While the central theme in Michiels's teaching might be understanding and respecting different points of view, the central theme in Jones's seems to have been discipline and self-reliance. These themes were also central to their lives, and to the "prior knowledge" they brought with them to Mission Elementary. In this instance, the content of the reform as it was enacted at Mission Elementary included at least some portion of their personal histories—what they used to build understanding, enact the reforms, and defend their practices.

A TEACHER'S QUEST TO UNDERSTAND DIFFERENCES

A cluster of Alice Michiels's recollections surrounding her education, interests, and personal experience form an important theme in her life: that is, a
persistent, long-standing attraction to cultures different than her own, especially to Mexican culture and the Spanish language. During the year of my
observations, Alice Michiels was 36 years old. She was slightly built; had long,
blond hair, glasses, and a vivacious personality; and she repeatedly talked about
the importance of understanding or respecting different points of view:

> Each [culture] has its own cultural perspective, and we need to
> respect one another . . . we need to listen to one another. . . . The
> modern-day classroom in California does not have all Anglo students.
> They are a diverse group, and if the teacher is not trained, they are not
> going to know how to deal with [their students]. . . . Your attitude,
> where you came from, your cultural background—[all these] deter-
> mine the type of learner you will be and learners are different.

Michiels's comments here represent a theme in her teaching, and understanding differences has been a nearly lifelong quest. She has taken up this
quest with a passion and it may have complemented the central ideas in the
reforms, opened her mind to learning about them—first in language arts,
later in mathematics.

As long as Alice Michiels can remember, she has had an interest in Mexican culture, especially in learning fluent Spanish. In 1976, after taking 4 years
of Spanish—coursework that included Spanish camps in the summer—Michiels
traveled to Mexico. The trip was a high school graduation gift from her parents. There she remembers becoming even more captivated with the language
and culture of that country. But Michiels enrolled in science, not language
courses during her first year at a junior college. She especially loved chemis-
try and was counseled toward that as a major. Halfway into her course of study
at a California state university, she decided to become a teacher, a profession
in which she could use her Spanish and knowledge of Mexican culture. She
immersed herself in school, working overtime to make up her language credits. Michiels worked as an aide in a bilingual room mornings in exchange for
books and tuition, and was part of an immersion program in Mexico during
the summer. Since that time, Alice Michiels has traveled back to Mexico almost every year and has many friends there.

Michiels earned a B.A. in liberal studies with a bilingual emphasis and began
teaching in an inner-city elementary school that enrolled predominantly black
and Hispanic children. Two years later she began a master's program, and after
5 years earned a master's degree in Teaching English to Speakers of other Lan-

guages (TESOL). Her coursework was heavily infused with theory and research about learning in a second language and second-language acquisition.

The story of Michiels's honeymoon is one of several that illustrate the prominence of the multicultural theme in her life, her informal learning beyond formal education. After teaching Mexican-American elementary students for a few years, Michiels was determined to supplement her social studies unit with a richer depiction of Mexican history and culture. With a great deal of enthusiasm, she began to plan a research project located in Mexico. When the man she was dating proposed to her, Michiels told him "yes, but on the condition that we spend our honeymoon in Mexico." They did, and she spent much of it photographing Mayan ruins or reading about that ancient culture. She still uses the fruits of her work from that trip—a slide show of Mexican history and culture accompanied by children's stories—for her social studies lessons.

In one sense, Michiels's experiences were a resource for changing her practice in the direction of the reform. For example, one reason Michiels may have been so engaged in the reforms is that her lifelong concern for understanding other points of view melded nicely with the aspects of reforms related to cognitive learning theories. Michiels mentioned such theories in relation to her master's work. Some of the big ideas in the reforms—for example, the importance of connecting new information to what a student already understands; or the idea that learning is a matter of "making sense" of new material—are embedded in those theories that argue that the mind develops through culture and social interaction. These ideas seem to have resonated with Alice Michiels as themes in her profession and her life. Compared to the complexity in Michiels's perspective, Kate Jones seemed to live by a few simple principles.

QUESTIONING ASSUMPTIONS, CONSTRUCTING NEW PRACTICES

Kate Jones's practice and attitudes about teaching seem to have been filtered through a strong set of beliefs informed by her experience as a military wife, and later as the mother of a military man. Her life has been steeped in military norms, and she seemed convinced that one of the more prominent values of such a life—disciplined behavior—was a key principle to live by, as well as one to guide her teaching choices. From her timer—she allowed exactly 60 seconds for transitions between lessons—and her drills on "math facts" to the many rules that ordered classroom activities, Jones had a strong belief in the benefits of discipline on the lives of children. This was so not only for the "disadvantaged children," she taught, but for her own children and grandchildren as well.

A small woman in her early to mid-50s with graying hair and a somewhat stern manner, Jones repeatedly talked about motivating students—about the importance of fostering self-discipline and self-reliance in them. For example, she said:

> If I can see a child . . . accept responsibility for himself . . . figure out how to do things on his own and make good decisions, that's almost as important as learning how to read and write. . . . I think all children are self-motivated if you give them an incentive. And with my kids, competition is an incentive. Children of eight are very competitive . . . [I tell my students] "You be the best you can be. It's just like the army, folks. But be all that you can be."

Jones's comments here are telling, for they might be a pep talk to herself as easily as to her students. Discipline and self-reliance have seen Kate Jones through some trying times. And true to the principles she espouses, she has seized the times of her life—good and bad—and used them for personal growth.

She essentially raised her two sons by herself and has helped raise her grandsons. When her son divorced, she followed him to a U.S. Marine base in California near the MUSD to help with his two boys. In the early 80s Jones volunteered at her grandson's school, becoming an aide and a MUSD district secretary. Laura Mather met her and convinced her to go back to college to get a teaching certificate. Jones did so and was hired by Mather before the curriculum reform had made its way to Mission Elementary, just as it was beginning to take shape in California. When I arrived in her classroom in 1994, she had been teaching for 5 years. The oldest teacher in my subset, she was not the most experienced.

Tradition, self-reliance, and discipline were prominent themes in the meaning Jones constructed around curriculum policy, Title I reform, bilingual education, and her teaching. While Michiels was trying to understand the ways in which cultural backgrounds may affect different learning styles, for the most part Jones seemed to expect that all students would learn in the same, conventional way if they were disciplined and motivated.

But for all their differences, Kate Jones and Alice Michiels still had *some* aspects of their practice in common. In fact, despite the fierce competition of ideas in and around the school, all the teachers in this study had features of their practices in common—likely more than any one of them might have in common with teachers in a school not exposed to reform.

Two points about Kate Jones' behavior—the behavior of the least reformed teacher in the study—can shed light on what might account for this phenomenon. First, Jones's penchant—as a lifelong military wife and mother—

for "following the rules" prompted this quite conservative teacher to take a look at the new math adoption at the MUSD (near the end of the 1994–1995 school year). That new mathematics program was reasonably consistent with the mathematics framework and curriculum guides, which until that time she seemed to have ignored. She reported thinking she might like the new program. Furthermore, district guidelines or rules related to curriculum reform have informed Jones's practice, at least to some extent. For example, when she talked about all the writing she asked her students to do, she said, "In this district we have to keep portfolios for the students' records." She followed that district rule by encouraging her students to write for many purposes—a practice consistent with reforms—and collecting varied samples for the students' portfolios.

But a second important point about Kate Jones's behavior related to curriculum reform is that she may have also learned—or opened her mind enough about her teaching to consider changing her practice—because of ongoing arguments with her *compañera*, Alice Michiels. Here conflict may have been a resource for change. By the end of the study, Jones was beginning to change her mind about the mathematics reforms, and even to think about adopting more practices consistent with the literacy curriculum reforms. For example, she had decided to "throw out the textbook" in the following year and use only literature from the library to teach reading and writing—something her partner had been doing for a couple of years. This was a major change in practice for Jones and it may have been due to Michiels, who reported trying to "teach my partner different ways to think about literacy." Michiels talked about the first year these two teachers "teamed" in the Compañero project at Mission: "My partner would stand up in the class and just read from the textbook and wonder why nobody was interested and losing every kid in the class. . . . So your kids just don't want to learn? No no no [I'd say] it is the way that you are teaching it." Here Michiels was commenting on Jones' ESL instruction during which the two teachers "mixed" their students. Jones later reported: "You know, textbooks can be deadly dull."

Michiels reported another challenge to Jones' assumptions about literacy instruction at the beginning of their second year together. She said: "My partner still has all her old phonics tapes and she uses those in the classroom because she finds it effective. . . . So I [tell her] I don't think you want to throw it out. I think you just need to contextualize it a little more." In these comments, Michiels is pressing Jones more toward the "reformed" end of the continuum by suggesting she "contextualize" her phonics lessons. This notion is bound up with "whole language" theory, or integrated language arguments that say children should learn lower-level skills in the context of learning to use language effectively. By midyear Michiels was reporting some demands she was making on Jones related to her ESL instruction and their "mixed-group lessons." She reported: "Because . . . in third grade . . . I am forcing it. I am making her do it that way . . . we are doing a lot of teaming . . . a lot of mixing of the students." There were more reports from Michiels in which she recounted challenging Jones on matters of teaching and learning, usually pressing her to consider an aspect of the reforms—in mathematics as well as in literacy.

There is evidence that Kate Jones was listening to Alice Michiels. For example, when asked how she managed to learn about ESL on the job (she had no preparation for teaching literacy or English to second language learners in her teacher education program), Jones reported: "For one, you've got a partner like Alice (laughs). . . . And Alice will guide you along slowly and patiently. . . . But we, together, try to build the English from where the range of our students' needs begin." Though the evidence does not suggest that Alice Michiels was "patient" in her dealings with Kate Jones, there are several other examples of Jones apparently paying attention to Michiels. And after repeatedly having her assumptions challenged, Kate Jones was beginning to change her mind about some long-held beliefs. That change of mind may in turn have been changing the way she thought about or responded to ideas in the curriculum reforms.

For instance, Jones talked one day at the beginning of the year, without prompting, about unquestioned authority versus "critical thinking." The views she expressed were not only atypical for her, but they were offered in the context of talking about Alice Michiels's practice:

Alice has been teaching . . . students [that] you don't have to agree. . . . All of our lives we're taught to get along and conform, which is wonderful if it works. But sometimes . . . you should be free to say, look, you have your right to your opinion but I don't . . . go along with that and here is why. . . . So we tried it in our room. . . . I think I have the . . . responsibility of teaching the children to not always agree. . . . Maybe to question.

This kind of talk goes against the grain of Jones's more typically "military-like" attitudes about discipline, rules, and obedience to authority. Here she is more ambivalent about matters of authority and even teaching. But more important, Jones seems to have connected at least some of her questions about authority to her literacy teaching.

It is here, in her thinking about language arts practices, that she produces something new that may have emerged from her conflicts with Michiels. She continued from her comments above:

That's why I am trying to get [my students] to judge and compare what they read [from other sources]. I make them question the stories

that are in that book . . . if they grow up believing everything that
somebody tells them, they're gonna get into trouble. . . . So I started to
question [this year]. I [said to them] I want you to question. I think
that's OK. You have that right.

Here, Jones does not talk explicitly about wanting students to justify claims
using reasoned arguments or textual evidence. But while she does not seem
to have yet made the connection between authority and argument, or authority
and disciplinary knowledge per se, Jones may be moving closer to the kind
of classroom discourse that the literacy reformers envision; that is, a discourse
that requires all students to use language persuasively, to think rigorously,
and to communicate effectively.

Likewise, Michiels seemed to have been watching and listening to Jones
as well as arguing with her about teaching practice. Near the end of the school
year, in the midst of reporting that she and Jones could no longer work together because it was too frustrating, Michiels digressed to report that she
had actually learned from Jones, even as she was trying to change her:

> Because she's really a mathematically powerful person. She does math
> a lot [and] she's very good in math. I don't think she realizes that a lot
> of students don't have that power, and so she can model. She doesn't
> realize but I tell her . . . and I got some ideas from her. You know the
> ways she asks and the kinds of questions she asks are really good . . .
> when you get to . . . watch each other teach, you pick things out. You
> can tell each other what you're doing . . . I get a chance to share ideas
> and we can help each other be better teachers, actually.

Here and in the earlier examples, conflict may have been productive as school
staff responded to curriculum policy ideas in the daily work of classroom
practice. Though these two teachers argued to the point of disbanding their
partnership, their disagreements prompted Michiels to think about her practice, to defend it, and perhaps revise it—all potentially productive activities.
In Jones's case especially, Michiels may have supplied the pressure Jones
needed to invest in the work of changing. When it came to mathematics, Alice
Michiels was in a position to provoke disequilibrium and challenge Jones's
assumptions more than the school's instructional leaders.

At the end of the school year, the second year of my study, Jones's earlier, dismissive attitude toward the mathematics reform had changed. She
reported, "When I saw what you actually do with these things [mathematics
adoption materials], I can live with all of this." A closer look at Jones's mathematics practice over time shows some of the details in her transition from

traditional methods toward a more reformed conception of mathematics teaching and learning.

A TEACHER IN TRANSITION

Comparing Jones's mathematics instruction at the beginning of the school year with that at the end of it illustrates not just a change of mind, but an observable change in her practice, which may also be due in part to her conflict with Michiels (and in part to her reading of the new math adoption at the MUSD, as noted earlier). Here is Kate Jones commenting about her practice at the beginning of the school year: "When I can get a child to do 200 math problems in 30 minutes and cry 'cause I'm making him stop, I'm almost there. . . . I just sit back and watch." Observations confirmed Jones's sense of successful mathematics instruction and achievement, which in her comments above, and the notes below, seems a good distance away from the reforms on any continuum of behavior or belief one might construct.

The two brief excerpts of Jones's practice below are taken from field notes at the beginning of the school year, and at midyear.

> The room is quiet, all children are facing the front, pencils in hand. They are working one and two-digit subtraction problems. There are seventy-two problems on the page. The room is almost silent now, except for the very quiet rustling of paper now and then, or the sound of a pencil lightly touching the desks. Occasionally, children hold up a hand and count their fingers. . . . Nine-fifteen a bell sounded the end of working on worksheets. Kate said, "You have one minute to read and work the story problem. You have one minute, start now." A minute later, Jones called up a girl to work the problem on the board. The room was still silent. Jones broke the silence to say "a smart third grader will always write the big number first" as the girl wrote the algorithm for the story problem on the board.
>
> (8/94)

> Jones started a timer after asking "okay are you ready." Then, click, "you are on your own." The children are all facing the front of the room. It is very quiet—all are writing. . . . Now at nine a.m., as more children finish their work, a few begin to chatter softly. Jones says, "There is no talking we're in a test setting." At 9:04 a.m., Jones says to the group, "You have one minute." Her comments elicit some sharp intakes of breath from a few kids. One minute later, at 9:05, the

buzzer goes off and Jones says "you have five minutes to study . . .
before the biggie." Jones's warning of the impending test seems to
propel the children into action. Some pull out their words, papers fly,
desks slam, a few begin to chatter with their neighbors . . . Jones says,
"shhhhh. I don't understand the talking." They quiet immediately.

(3/95)

These excerpts of Kate Jones's classroom, along with her comments just above
and earlier, show the fast-paced, disciplined, drill-oriented aspects of her
mathematics teaching. These characteristics of her practice are far from the
instruction and curriculum envisioned by reformers. While at this point in the
story, most other teachers in my subset were trying out the reforms and attending trainings, Kate Jones was resisting them. She reported, "When the
teachers first got it [samples of the new mathematics program,] I thought,
'Oh, my God we're going to play ourselves to death.'" And many of her comments noted earlier were consistent with this negative review of the reforms.

But the last time I observed Jones, near the end of the year, she was
allowing her students to spend quite a bit of time "explaining their thinking" to the class, about how they solved a problem she posed to them. This
approach—consistent with Michiels's desire to understand and build on what
her students knew—was one that Alice Michiels had used and talked about
for some time. Michiels had learned about this particular practice at a county
in-service on the mathematics frameworks. A short excerpt from Jones's math
lesson on the idea of patterns (in this instance, multiples of nine) follows:

J: "Well I have a much harder pattern here" pointing to the second
     row of numbers—27, 36, 45, ____, ____. "F (an Hispanic boy),
     what's our next number going to be?"

F: 54 (very softly)

J: And our next number?

F: 63 (with more confidence in his voice)

J: How in the world did you figure that one out?

F: Because 27 and then 36 is like going up and then down. Because
     27, that's a small number and a big number. And, 36, is a bigger
     number and a smaller number.

J: Does anyone else have another way to figure it out. R [another
     Hispanic boy]? What did you come up with?

R: 9 times 5 is 45. And 9 times 6 is 54. And 9 times 7 is 63.

J: So he used the 9 multiplication facts to get it. B [a poor, Caucasian
     boy, whose father is in jail], talk to me.

B: 1 to the 2 is 3 and then take away 1 from the 7 which is 6. And just
     kept on doing it.

Jones demonstrated how this might work on the board—adding 1 to the 10s and taking 1 away from the 1s. Then she said, "That's great! I would have done it the same way." They continued with several other patterns and Jones made comments—for example, "Anyone else do it differently?" Or, "Give her some thinking time; don't rush her." Then she asked the students to work on their own to construct number patterns. She called up several of them to write their patterns on the board and have the class figure out the pattern. She ended by explaining: "If you learn one little corner of a number pattern, you can really go."

(Field note, 6/95)

This lesson, while perhaps not a model of rigorous mathematics reform, is nevertheless quite a contrast to the other two lessons from earlier in the year. This lesson differs from the others in several respects. First, children in the lesson just above are not silent, while those in the first two examples for the most part were. Second, Jones appeared to encourage the students not only to talk, but to listen to one another, and she also appeared to be listening to her students carefully. Third, Jones encouraged students to "take time to think" as opposed to challenging them to race through as many algorithms as possible in the earlier lessons.

In this lesson, Jones was moving a bit closer to the mathematics reforms in California at the time of this study, and to research that suggests students can learn "cognitive strategies" when such reasoning processes are made public (Porter, 1991). California's 1987 mathematics model curriculum guide stressed that "listening to others affords [students] the opportunity to contemplate the thinking of others and to consider the implications for their own understanding" (California State Department of Education, 1987b, p. 14). Researchers have argued that teachers and students can model alternative approaches for attacking a problem and students can help "scaffold" tasks for one another. From the view of reform, not only should students be actively engaged in discussing math ideas, but teachers should probe and listen for clues to understanding. Jones was not only encouraging her students to talk a bit—something very unusual in her classroom—but based on her interview comments, she was actually beginning to listen to her students and was pleasantly surprised by the range of strategies they employed.

In the later lesson, Jones was also encouraging students to take some *time to think* about the problems she had set up for them. This, too, was in contrast to her earlier practice, in which she pressed students to arrive at a memorized answer or use computation procedures swiftly. And this aspect of her instruction was also closer to the reform vision. While children in high-poverty schools have tended to spend a good deal of time on computational tasks (Zucker, 1991), the mathematics curriculum guide in California wanted *all* students to "make sense" of arithmetic operations by connecting big ideas—for example, patterns—to them. Jones was in this territory—the "patterns and functions strand" of the state model curriculum—when she asked her students to predict the numbers in a pattern, then explain their "rule" for arriving at an answer. For Jones, the examples described here are all moves toward the more reformed kind of practice Michiels had been trying to implement for some time.

While Jones was mustering the will to learn more about the reforms, in part because of pressure from her teammate and district policy, she needed more support to develop her capacity for practicing in the way of the mathematics reforms. Here would have been a perfect opportunity for a knowledgeable, easily accessible mentor of the sort described earlier to help Jones build on what she was learning in her classroom, for example, by using the literature on children's thinking and problem solving (Peterson, Fennema, & Carpenter, 1991), or by helping Jones understand more about the nature of mathematics (Ball, 1991; Porter, 1991). Though Michiels provided Jones with some thoughtful observations of her instruction, she was struggling with the reforms herself, and was unable to serve as an authoritative mentor. When it came to the mathematics reform, she could *challenge* Jones, but not *support* her further or deeper learning.

CONCLUSION

In the case of Alice Michiels and Kate Jones, conflict was both counterproductive and productive. Competing school and district messages—about the importance of CTBS and the CLAS results, for example—together with Jones's success in using methods that conflicted with what Michiels was trying to learn, combined to heighten Alice Michiels's ambivalence about her reformed practices. That ambivalence between the old reliable practices she had used to build her sense of efficacy and the new untried and perhaps untrue practices she was working to invent, undermined her will to progress with the reforms. However, the many conflicts of conviction between Michiels and Jones also prompted Michiels to think about her practice and to defend it, perhaps alter it in light of her reflection, all of which can be productive aspects of professional development. Further, such conflicts, by repeatedly challenging deeply held assumptions, opened Jones to change, and to the possibility of learning about reformed practices. But both teachers were coping with conflict with too few social resources to sustain and deepen their reformed practice. Such resources at the school were limited by inherited conceptions of work norms, which allowed teachers to practice with autonomy, choosing among disparate goals and means, and by the lack of sustained opportunities for learning with knowledgeable others.

The case of Jones and Michiels demonstrates potential for the reforms, reason for reformers to hope, as well as problems or obstacles to the instructional reforms growing in schools. First, even Kate Jones, the most traditional teacher in my subset, was rethinking her practice by the end of the study. That seems to indicate reason for optimism. Here, conflict was in part a productive change mechanism. It was embedded in a process that included a competition of ideas, challenge, negotiation, and adjustments in belief or practice. The conflict between Jones and Michiels was in the direction of professional interaction, the norm that research and theory suggest can be a source of learning as well as a means of accountability. While Jones was "pressured" to try out the reforms by her own penchant for "following the rules," she also had her assumptions challenged by her teammate.

This discordant and adaptive process is also consistent with the idea that "belief can follow action" (Weick, 1979). Due to pressure from district policy and her teammate, Kate Jones tried new instructional practices which in turn intrigued her, prompting her to embrace at least some of the new ideas and take further steps. For example, after encouraging her students to talk about their solutions to problems, listening carefully to them, and then using their thinking to instruct them, Jones reported feeling less resistant to the reforms. Her trial reform-oriented practices and her students' responses to those practices breached the classroom routine, created cognitive dissonance, and became an incentive for further change (Kennedy, 1991).

On the other hand, the reforms faced obstacles to becoming more deeply rooted in the practices of these teachers. Limited social resources at the school and mixed messages from the district diminished the impact of the curriculum policy and the challenges to Jones's assumptions. These same factors undermined Michiels's fledgling change attempts. At the point when her internal motivation to change seemed high, Kate Jones needed more instructional support of the sort outlined earlier in this chapter in order to develop her capacity for actually moving further in the direction of the reforms—especially the mathematics reforms. So did Alice Michiels.

A problem here was that the interaction and debate between Jones and Michiels was restricted as a productive reform mechanism, first by the school's changing, but still somewhat private work norms. It was restricted further by mixed messages from high-stakes assessments and the still unspecified meaning of mathematics reform. Jones and Michiels's debate, as a productive lever for change, was confined further still by what these two teachers brought to the task of reforming their practices.

While the school culture was beginning to change, the norms were not yet conducive to teacher consultations and joint work on the core issues of practice. Thus, the debate between Jones and Michiels did not range out far enough into the school, nor did it tap into the school's subject matter expert—

that is, the representative on the mathematics curriculum committee. The former would have provided more accountability: the pressure of collective staff expectations as a means to judge Jones's or Michiels's personal instructional preferences. The latter could have been the sort of "credible and easily accessible technical assistance" that has been reported to help teachers change— someone to provide advice on concrete problems of daily practice. In addition to the problem of norms, Mission's mathematics specialist had full classroom teaching responsibilities and not much time for mentoring. Committee work took still more of his time. So more financial resources to release him to spend more time as a mathematics mentor in the school could have helped in this situation.

On a related point, because the norms of interdependent work were still weak in this school, and because the district was sending mixed messages about performance goals, the mathematics reforms were still quite open to a wide range of interpretations. Conflicting high stakes tests gave Kate Jones a legitimate warrant to continue to resist reforms and tended to diminish the impact of Michiels's challenges to her practice. So Jones, while pressured to some extent to try reformed practices, was still reasonably free to choose from an array of instructional ideas in competition with them. Likewise, conflicting messages and Jones's promise of student outcomes served to heighten Michiels's ambivalence about the changes she was struggling to make in her practice.

Furthermore, these teachers brought only a portion of the understanding and instructional capacity they would have needed to change their practice: Jones was comfortable and capable with mathematics content, but her conception of authority and the nature of mathematical knowledge led her to consider learning a matter of reproducing "the facts." Michiels was uneasy with mathematics—she lacked a strong sense of efficacy—but she understood a good deal about cognitive learning theory, her students, and how to teach them to understand subject matter (in language arts and science). A culture of staff interdependence and continuous interaction, along with consistent messages about instructional goals, could have been a more powerful force for transforming the differences in these two teachers into opportunities for learning.

Although they were at quite different places in their response to curriculum reform—in terms of when and to what extent they had been persuaded to change their practices—both Kate Jones and Alice Michiels needed more coherent guidance in order to move beyond where they were. This was especially so in mathematics. Neither Laura Mather nor her deputies were prepared to provide that guidance in mathematics (though in literacy as it was bound up with bilingual education, they were more prepared). And the school mathematics mentor appeared to have little time to do so.

While Michiels was struggling to change her mathematics teaching to square with the CLAS, Louise James was reporting in the fall of 1994 that "the CLAS is dead." That fledgling assessment, as well as the kind of curriculum and instruction it represented, had met with popular and political opposition. The governor was withholding funds; Laura Mather was reporting meetings with angry parents—parents who argued the assessment was invading their children's privacy. By the time the no-nonsense Kate Jones was becoming less resistant to curriculum reform and could have used some help, the agreement over systemic reform in California was breaking down even more. The new state superintendent appointed task forces charged with incorporating more basic skills into California's curriculum. The demise of the CLAS and the state shifts toward basic skills coincided with the federal call for more rigorous intellectual conceptions of achievement. Thus, Kate Jones, Alice Michiels, Anita Lorenz, and Monique Ponds were left wrestling with the problem of what to do next, in a context of political turmoil not uncommon in American education. Likewise, Laura Mather, Louise James, and other school leaders had to make difficult decisions on school-wide reform issues in the same incoherent environment. In Chapter 5, I return to the school level to take up one of those decisions and the conflict that erupted as the staff moved from planning to action.

Clarity, Complexity, and Collaboration: The Technical and Social Tensions of Transforming Policy into Practice

The circumstances leading up to a significant staff decision to take on further reform, and the circumstances following it, show how Mission's staff coped with the tensions in reform ideals over time. The staff had to manage the tension between the complex ambiguity inherent in practicing the curriculum reforms, and the ideal of clear school level goals. Likewise, they had to manage tensions between a commitment to the ideal of clarity and the ideal of collaboration. Finally, collectively the staff had to manage with few of the social or conventional resources they needed to support their commitment to further change. Mission's story illustrates the critical role that organizational learning, identity, and professional growth can play in putting reforms into practice. The staff was trying to overcome deeply rooted norms of autonomy and personal or professional experience that were in some instances inconsistent with the reforms—all without much external guidance to help them.

The difficulty of putting the key reform ideals into practice was compounded by a contentious political climate and by long-standing arguments throughout the American educational system. The school and community embodied many of those arguments in their student population and in the strongly held beliefs of their staff, parents, or district personnel. Thus, enacting these reforms was not simply a technical matter for school leaders and educators: The process involved managing in the face of personal and social conflict as well. Conflicting policy purposes and professional identities interacted in the ongoing school renewal process.

THE DECISION TO RESTRUCTURE AND ITS AFTERMATH: INVENTING PRACTICE FROM PRINCIPLES

Several points are important to review about Mission Elementary's response to reforms *before* the staff decision to restructure their Title I program and school mission. First is the staff's general commitment to the organizational, curricular, and instructional reforms—that is, high academic standards for all students. Title I instruction was less fragmented than it had been before the 1988 amendments, as the staff had for the most part integrated that instruction into the reform-oriented classroom curriculum. Second is the difficult, uncertain, and complex performances such a commitment entailed, especially when many of the students were poor, limited-English-speaking children, and bilingual education goals were added to an already complicated mix of ideas. The curriculum reforms were only partially specified; the complex performances they required of both teachers and students were not easily reduced to a list of "best practices" or represented in the aggregate.

Third, before the staff's decision to restructure, inherited conceptions of work or leadership norms, together with conflicting messages in the school and its environment, constrained capacity for change and diluted potential capacity building resources. On the latter point, reforms were competing with other aims the district and school staff found compelling. A vague school mission allowed a wide range of interpretations of a myriad of program ideas in the school. On the former point, despite sharing ideas, coordinating some instruction in small grade-level teams, and making collaborative school-wide decisions about resources, teachers were more *independent* than *interdependent* when it came to specific teaching goals and means, especially across grade levels.

Finally, during the period of time in which Mission's staff was deciding to restructure and then actually trying to implement its changes, the CLAS became caught up in political cross fire. But while the ambitious curriculum reforms were under attack in California, they were embraced at the federal level, and joined by a more technical component: a renewed and rigorous press during the reauthorization of Title I (tied to Goals 2000) for coherence—clear, common goals and data driven, school-level planning ("School wide Programs," Sec. 114, *Chapter 1 Handbook*, USDE, November 1994). Here, some technical guides were available to schools, though mostly in list form and "in principle." For example, the school-wide projects "idea book" points out that "many projects are designed on the basis of 'effective schools' correlates. . . ." Two key principles include collaborative planning and a "clear and focused school mission" (Pechman & Feister, 1994). More important was the lack of support for school leadership or teachers to learn about merging these different ideals of the reform—clarity, complexity, and collaboration—in workable, school-level, and classroom practices.

Making the Decision to Change

In the spring of 1994, Laura Mather was feeling the pressure of competing aims which, at the district level, had been pushing schools to gear up for the CLAS, but also wanted them to raise CTBS scores. First, Mather was especially concerned because her school's mathematics scores on the CLAS were the second lowest in the district (though scores were very low state-wide). And second, Mather was troubled by a small study that Mark Bills, her district supervisor, had asked her and other principals to conduct using not the CLAS, but the CTBS scores. Mather reported that after studying her school's CTBS scores, "I couldn't tell Mark that the students who stayed at Mission for four years scored better than those who did not." Mark Bills visited Mission Elementary in light of the low scores. He told Mather he saw some good things going on in classrooms, but the staff at Mission didn't seem to be working toward a common goal, from his perspective. He told Mather to work on raising the scores in mathematics. An important point to note here is that during this time of concern about test scores, both Mather and her Title I coordinator reported that Mission's scores on the reading and writing portion of the CLAS were "average or above" for the district. But that information seemed to have been lost in the worry over the math CLAS scores and the all-around low CTBS scores.

Mather reported that Bills's assessment was likely correct: even though teachers had agreed upon a school mission, they did not have a common understanding of the mission; they were "going off in all directions" and "doing their own thing." In April, when staff at Mission Elementary met to plan for the following year, change in the Title I program was at the top of the agenda for Laura Mather and Louise James. Mather shared the comparative CTBS scores with her staff, and they all agreed that Title I, as it was then configured in the school, did not seem to make a difference in their students' scores. That meeting, together with planning for a Goals 2000 grant, contributed to a major staff decision to restructure the Title I program by first developing a more collaborative, commonly understood school mission: that is, in Little's (1990) terms, by moving in the direction of "mutual obligation" for school goals, toward interdependence and away from independence. Second, over the span of a few months during the process of planning for the Goals 2000 grant, staff developed an even narrower, technically coherent goal which, for political as well as technical reasons, became, in effect, raising CTBS scores in reading.

Mather and James had been trying to build agreement for change, and initially the decision to restructure Title I around a narrower (less vague), more commonly held vision—"literacy by the end of first grade"—was by all accounts collaborative: All staff agreed to the new plan and helped to design it. First, staff decided to concentrate all Title I resources in the early grades—kindergarten, first, and second—in order both to prevent later learning problems and serve the narrowed, school-wide focus of literacy by the end of grade one. (See Pinnell, 1990 and Slavin, Karweit, & Wasik, 1991, for more on the idea of early intervention.) Upper grade teachers—led by a third- grade teacher whom Mather had hired—offered to give up their Title I resources to the primary grades, reasoning that they would benefit in the long run by inheriting students who could read. The third-, fourth-, and fifth-grade teachers gave up their space, aides, and Title I teachers.

Next, Mather asked the kindergarten teachers to work for an hour each day with Title I first graders in order to provide those students with some continuity from kindergarten to first grade, and again, to serve the new school focus of "literacy." Mather reported that she also wanted the kindergarten teachers to have a better sense of the academic expectations of first grade teachers. Here her concern was to have teachers work more interdependently across grade levels. With a minimal amount of debate, kindergarten teachers agreed to help first-grade teachers, and the staff seemed on their way to embracing a collaborative attitude across grade levels. Mather and James were ebullient, and likened the planning meeting and the new Title I plan to a "religious experience." Every report by Mather, James, and staff alike suggested that the new school vision was shared, the plan was collaboratively constructed and, for the most part, camaraderie reigned in the school.

But that state of affairs at Mission Elementary School turned out to be an idyllic interlude. Much of the work entailed in this staff decision to change would be an entirely new experience for Mission's staff. So when Kate Jones was still resisting the mathematics reforms at the end of the 1993–1994 school year, Mission Elementary was in the midst of a momentous decision that would begin to change radically the staff's daily work, and thus a portion of their lives. It would change the fabric of the school's social relations—pressing teachers to challenge one another and defend their practices that had, for the most part, previously been unquestioned. It would ask for sacrifices from upper-grade teachers and students in the service of a collective goal. And those sacrifices, in part due to Mission's transient students, would become more difficult than many staff seemed to understand at the time of the meeting. Finally, the decision to restructure would challenge established routines and personally held beliefs about the nature of teaching, curriculum, and learning. Neither the workshops on reform that Mather attended, nor the reform documents she later encountered detailed or dwelled much on the social conflict that can burst out of the contradiction and ambivalence of change (Marris, 1974). Mather had to manage that conflict with little support or guidance over the course of the 1994–1995 school year.

Goal Clarity and Collaboration

Though the new plan represented a significant staff attempt to move toward school-level coherence—goal clarity and collaborative work informed by "student performance data"—it had increased the potential for conflict on two fronts: First, the new school mission would not accommodate as much variation in interpretation, because it was much more specific than the earlier, vague mission. Second, the "mutual obligation" or "interdependence" among the staff, especially kindergarten, first-, and second-grade teachers, also increased, thus intensifying the potential for conflict. After the decision, teachers at Mission Elementary had to interact more often. They had to talk about and come to some understanding of varying opinions about the meaning of their decision to change the school's Title I program. Though Anita Lorenz reported daily interaction with peers over core teaching issues during her teacher education, for many at Mission, this kind of work norm was a radical departure from past experience.

Laura Mather's new leadership stance was another factor that likely contributed to the social conflict at Mission. To move her staff toward change, she imposed some portion of the new plan, or at least used her authority more than was her usual style. Mather really pressed the norm of "joint work" among teachers across grade levels because she wanted kindergarten teachers to provide tutoring to their former students, now in first grade and struggling to read. While it might have been difficult to disagree in the midst of a large group, it seems likely that several of the kindergarten teachers were not happy with the new arrangement.

Finally, the staff had to manage the trade-offs in their coherent response to reform—concentrating resources and prioritizing goals to focus on improving literacy in the lower grades—because of practical constraints in the school (limited funding, for one, a transient student body, for another). At least some of the conflict that grew out of the new Title I plan would have been avoided had there been more financial resources available to the staff—that is, enough funding to hire quality personnel so that the upper grades could have received support as well as the lower grades.

Below, I explore three instances of social conflict that ensued from the decision to restructure: First, beginning in early fall, most kindergarten teachers resisted aspects of the new plan, especially those that required extra effort and time on their part. Conflict erupted in a series of emotionally charged meetings and union intervention. Second, the primary grade teachers disagreed on the meaning of developmental education and curriculum standards, and thus over how to use their newfound assets. Finally, with newly arriving students unable to read, the upper grade teachers began to feel the loss of their resources—they wanted help now, not later. Their choice to forgo Title I resources in the service of a coherent school plan had consequences for their students—consequences that became much more clearly defined once they were living with them.

Collaboration and Dissension

In September, one month after the new plan began at Mission, conflict erupted when kindergarten teachers—all but Anita Lorenz, who had recently transferred to that grade from second grade—filed a grievance with their union over Mather's insistence that they work an extra hour in first grade in exchange for an extra Title I aide. The district contract now has several paragraphs— coined the "Miss Laura" section by Mather's principals group—defining what a principal can or cannot ask a kindergarten teacher to do. Anita Lorenz's recalcitrance in that union matter resulted in a name-calling session at a staff meeting. Another kindergarten teacher accused Lorenz of capitulating to extra demands; she called Lorenz a wimp for doing so. According to several reports, Lorenz was angry, disagreed with the other teachers, and reported thinking the new plan to follow students across kindergarten and first grades was "important." Furthermore, she interpreted the new plan to mean the early primary teachers—kindergarten and first—should be mutually responsible for the new school goal of literacy by the end of the first grade, in exchange for their extra resources. She reported: "There are too many people who gave up their rights to have an aide and [other resources] . . . for the people [in primary grades] not to be accountable."

But other kindergarten teachers disagreed with Lorenz and Laura Mather at a September staff meeting where the conflict escalated. Mather reported on that meeting: "It was so bad. They were being so mean to Anita." Mather explained that the kindergarten teachers were angry because Anita was the first to try the new plan and had used the teacher meeting to report "it's working fine for me." Mather continued her account of the meeting:

> That was the wrong thing to say because they didn't want it to
> happen. So it got real nasty. . . . I was so angry. I slammed my hand
> down on the table and said, "That's it, I have had enough. I thought
> we could try to make this work for the good of the students." . . . My
> voice caught and I got up and I stormed across the room, went into
> Louise's office, slammed the door, sat down in her chair, and started
> to cry.

One of Anita Lorenz's friends reported that Lorenz told her the meeting "was brutal, really brutal." These, and several similar accounts, provide a window on just how emotionally and politically charged the process of educational reform can be. These are not simply technical matters for school leaders: They involve personal and social quandaries as well.

But these accounts also illustrate aspects of the new norms some reformers are pressing for regarding teachers—norms of professionalism. True to her declaration that she did not want to work in isolation, Anita Lorenz seemed quite willing to take professional responsibility for a shared goal with the first-grade teachers—that is, the goal of ensuring that all students could read and write by the end of first grade. Remember, she had even talked to the first-grade teachers about a similar goal when she was still teaching second grade. Then she had pressed her colleagues to "make it a goal that all . . . children can write a complete sentence when they come into my class at the beginning of the year." Now, as a new kindergarten teacher, she was sticking with that professional stance; that is, "to team with the other grade levels and the other people at my grade level." The sort of professional collegiality that Lorenz's attitudes show—collective responsibility for student learning—when it goes to the heart of instructional decisions and daily practice can improve the capacity of schools as well as that of individual teachers (Darling-Hammond, 1992b; Little, 1990; Sykes, 1990). It has also been found to improve student performance in some schools (Newmann & Wehlage, 1995; Purkey & Smith, 1983, 1985).

But just as teachers at Mission reported that cooperative work among students did not come naturally, so, too, have researchers found that teacher collaboration and public discussion focused on student learning does not happen naturally. Lorenz, for example, reported taking care to teach her students how to help one another on academic tasks. Students had to learn how to be productive in such learning groups. Teacher collaboration also "requires a great deal of organizational and individual learning" (Lieberman & Miller, 1992, p. 32). Teachers who move from the isolation of personal classroom decisions to a more professional, public arena have quite an adjustment to make. Still, the kindergarten teachers in this school (with the exception of Lorenz) seemed unwilling to consider a norm that would constrain their actions, even in the service of improving student achievement—at least, not quickly. They resorted to the authority of collective bargaining instead.

In this case, working less independently and clarifying goals meant confrontation. Laura Mather was not used to such confrontation with her staff. With more experience she might have tried to find some middle ground, some compromise during this series of emotional meetings. Or, had the school actually substituted "collective autonomy" (Little, 1990)—that is, school-based accountability—for the norm of individual autonomy, Mather may have had more room for productive action. In this latter instance, individual practices would be publicly considered as a routine matter. The authority of teachers—deliberating over defensible practices using the "good for students" standard

Mather evoked earlier—may have substituted for the clash of authority between the union and "management" that ensued here.

But in this latter instance, structural changes at the district and cultural changes at the school would have been necessary to bolster the rhetoric of "site-based management." At this point in the story, the former had not been considered (Mather was bound by district collective bargaining and union rules) and the latter—cultural change in the school—though under way, was in its early stages. Further, Laura Mather was learning about the difficulties of conflict and how to manage it productively, merely through on-the-job experience beginning in September. She had little or no "instruction" and no "curriculum" as guides. Such guides, in the form of an instructional conversation with veterans knowledgeable about school change, may have helped Mather guide her staff as they developed and enforced the norms of collective authority and professional practice. The social resources that could have supported such work were missing and Mather was trying to invent them.

Conflicts of Meaning

But the problems surrounding some teachers' resistance to the new plan wasn't the only conflict around. Clarifying the school goal and working less independently had also begun to surface teachers' conflicting interpretations of the meaning of that goal, thus making consensus more difficult than it was when the plan was first developed in April of the previous school year. First-grade and kindergarten teachers began to disagree openly over the meaning of developmental education and curriculum standards; therefore, they disagreed over the common goal they thought they had earlier agreed upon—literacy by the end of first grade—and what methods they might use to collaboratively achieve that goal. With the new, narrower, school-wide focus, teachers across grade levels had to confront their disagreements at the concrete level of day-to-day instructional decisions. This was a painful and difficult process.

For Juan Ramirez, a young Latino man, hired by Mather to teach first grade, the matter of his students' school success was worth the fight, no matter the pain and difficulty involved. He, unlike the kindergarten teachers, liked the new plan. But he vehemently disagreed with most of Mission's kindergarten teachers' conception of developmentally appropriate instruction and curriculum standards. At the end of the first year, he said:

> One thing that has been very very difficult this year is we're trying to work collectively kindergarten through second grade. . . . In essence [some kindergarten teachers] have become so accustomed to not teaching they don't want to teach . . . that's how I see it. I have a teacher who is sending me students saying that the instrument [Title I

assessment] is invalid because the material it covers hasn't been taught. [I said] "Then why am I wasting my time [screening Title I students] if [the curriculum] is not being taught and if you are not . . . doing your job? In other districts where I've taught [kindergarten], my kids at the end of their year were reading. Adding and subtracting. Here they know five vowels for God sake." . . . If looks could kill I would have been dead.

This emotionally charged disagreement illustrates the heightened potential for conflict when teachers move toward working more interdependently. Ramirez believed in a particular conception of literacy by the end of first grade. Now, under the new plan, he felt more dependent on the support of the kindergarten teachers to reach that goal. But he was dismayed to realize they did not agree with his conception of academic standards (what children should be able to do by the end of kindergarten and first grade) or developmental education (what methods are appropriate and when). He began to articulate the strong feelings he had about such matters in public meetings. By several reports, the kindergarten teachers felt just as strongly about their views.

In the comments just above and below, Ramirez articulates his sense of "high standards," developmental instruction, and a shared obligation for the new school goal of literacy. His comments show at least some portion of the kindergarten teachers' views as well. Because of these different convictions about teaching and standards, Ramirez didn't think the kindergarten teachers should receive the extra resources "if you're not going to be utilizing them the way they should be." Because, he said:

If the burden comes down on first grade . . . to create a group of kids that are literate, then I need to be supported by [kindergarten]. . . . I don't expect the kids to write a paragraph. But I do expect those kids [to] be reading and writing and subtracting. . . . [Some teachers] hide behind these buzz words "developmentally appropriate." Well, developmental means so much. [To me] it means that from day one you give [students] the opportunity to write and express themselves. As . . . [they] develop the ability to go from exploratory expression on paper . . . to conventional writing: that's developmental!

As for one of the kindergarten teachers who interpreted the developmental philosophy differently, Ramirez said: "Her standards just aren't high enough . . . I think that she expects too little. I think that she really doesn't challenge these kids enough, and, by the time I get them they're already a year behind."

In Ramirez's comments, one can see multiple conflicts of meaning between him and other teachers over competing instructional ideas—for example, grade-level standards and developmental methods. And, his struggle with the other teachers demonstrates the tension that can arise between goal clarity and staff collaboration. The drive toward goal clarity can make consensus more difficult; the lack of consensus can make collaboration more difficult. In this case, conflicts of interpretation surfaced as staff moved away from both their abstract school vision and the school norm of independence. Teachers began to disagree with each other over what developmentally appropriate means, and what to do about instruction in relation to that ideal. Teachers disagreed over the meaning of high academic standards and how best to work toward them. They disagreed over when to work toward them, and when children might be capable of mastering those standards. These are some of the same arguments that Anita Lorenz, Monique Ponds, and Alice Michiels were having—not with others, but with themselves.

Coping with conflict was embedded in the process of adapting policy ideals to practice at Mission Elementary. Here the social interaction of these teachers is beginning to move in the direction of a new norm for this school—a norm that requires public debate over practices and beliefs in order to integrate and defend them. This process has the potential to create social resources for change—for example, mutual understanding, consistent expectations for student performances, and professional accountability to one another for those performances. Such social resources can become a kind of scaffolding for teaching and teacher learning. In the latter instance, teachers can instruct one another and press for thoughtful defense of ideas and practice. In the former instances, teachers can contribute to one another's efficacy through mutual obligation to students throughout the school. But inventing radical new norms without some guidance is not easy, and is not without pitfalls. As in the case of Alice Michiels and Kate Jones, the debate between these teachers holds the potential to be counterproductive as well as productive.

Practical Constraints

A final instance of school-level conflict that emerged after the staff decision to restructure shows how the difficulty of melding reform ideals in practice—already considerable—is compounded by practical constraints (in this instance, only modest financial resources and a transient student body). Initially, when devising their new school plan, the staff reasoned their Title I students were not going to "catch up," based on the comparative CTBS scores Mather and James had shown them. Staff also based their judgments on research evidence, arguing for a concentrated effort at prevention over later remedial work. Here is a seemingly rational, data-driven and research-based decision on the part of a staff working together in the service of a clear school-wide goal—all part of the coherence and collaboration ideals pressed by reforms.

But it didn't take long for the upper-grade teachers to learn that the practical consequences of the plan were not to their liking. Teachers of third, fourth, and fifth grades began to feel they couldn't wait for the positive results of their long-range collaborative planning—that is, of finally getting students who could read. One reason was that new students who transferred into Mission were sometimes unable to read, though they were old enough to be placed in the upper grades. The upper grade teachers wanted help now. By midyear, they began to complain at staff meetings. Alice Michiels, the third-grade bilingual teacher who agreed to the plan even though she lost her resources, felt the loss well before midyear. She reported that the weaknesses in the plan were apparent immediately:

> We had no help in the upper grades and we were feeling really frustrated, trying to do everything [by ourselves] and having . . . kids that were like fish out of water, obviously not functioning. We could have sent them back [to second grade] but that's really hard on their self-esteem.

In this instance the staff at Mission had to manage the trade-offs between a plan that melded the reform ideals (coherence and collaboration) and the school's practical problems (too few financial resources and a transient student body). An important point here is that staff choices or strategies made at the school level had complex consequences for students at the classroom level, thus compounding the difficulty of managing the dilemmas the staff encountered. I take up this topic further in Chapter 6, in which I explore the trade-offs for Title I students in the staff's new plan to restructure.

Collaborative work and clear goals are compelling policy ideals, informed by social science research. But Laura Mather and her staff had the very difficult task of managing the tensions that can arise from trying to meld these policy ideals in practice. They were also wrestling with divergent conceptions of professional norms, which the decision to restructure forced them to confront. In the first instance, the traditional norm of collective bargaining was pitted against the norm of professional accountability to peers when the loss of individual choice was apparently too costly to some kindergarten teachers. In the second instance, the staff was moving out of the isolation of the classroom into the arena of professional debate. Here again, the norm of individual preference was challenged by teachers who had committed to a mutual goal, but who could not agree with colleagues over the meaning of that goal. Ramirez took seriously his responsibility to improve the performance of all his students, but felt he was dependent upon other teachers to accomplish his goal. He could not accept the performance of some colleagues, and confronted them over issues at the heart of their practices. Like Anita Lorenz, his behavior is unusual when compared to that of teachers in most schools.

In the third instance, teachers who had sacrificed for the collective goal of improving all students' literacy skills—also a new norm in this school where equitable distribution of resources had been standard practice—found it very difficult to watch particular students flounder every day (another sort of professional norm—that is, responsibility to their own individual students). While the former (personal sacrifice for the potential larger good) contributes to coherent planning and is sound in principle, the latter (a desire to respond to the needs of individual students) is a powerful influence on teachers (Jackson, 1968; Lipsky, 1980; Lortie, 1975)—and with good reason. Teaching is an interpersonal profession. Together, Mather, Lorenz, Ramirez, Michiels, and a few other teachers that Mather had hired were introducing a new notion of what it means to teach into Mission Elementary; and in doing so, they had the potential to enrich the school's capacity for change. But the need to manage or cope with conflict was integral to the new social arrangements they were creating.

Mather pressed forward with the original plan the group had decided upon in April, despite the emotional conflict and lack of consensus. On the one hand, the decision to concentrate resources in the early grades, to clarify their goals, and to take mutual responsibility for them may have caused so much agitation that the school's social fabric was damaged, and the new mission along with it. Some teachers, mostly those Mather had inherited rather than hired, continued to resist it. On the other hand, if Laura Mather had waited for everyone on her staff to agree, the staff may have never moved forward with a coherent plan to improve achievement. Purkey and Smith (1985) cite workplace researchers who advise industry and business reformers "not to wait for everyone to agree with proposed changes" (p. 379). They suggest this approach recognizes that a certain amount of dissent and conflict can be healthy for an organization.

No matter the choices a school leader might make, there are trade-offs to manage. In the midst of the social turmoil that had erupted at Mission, Juan Ramirez had a solution that he shared with Mather:

> I say take a hike! Laura has talked about creating a magnet school with a common vision. . . . What do you do to get a forum of teachers who all believe in the same philosophy? You adopt a goal, a vision, and you start to structure your school to meet that vision. Those who do not want to participate in it, well the door swings both ways.

There is some evidence that Ramirez's revolutionary suggestion is sensible. Newmann and Wehlage found schools that had successfully restructured their organization and curriculum in the direction of reforms, and whose students' achievement improved based on "authentic" measures, were all either schools of choice (both for students and faculty) or newly formed charter schools. The staff in these schools viewed their freedom to select teachers who embraced the schools' vision as a key factor in their success. At Mission Elementary the work of inventing new norms required pressing for a shared commitment among a mix of staff who disagreed. The process was rife with conflict. It had both the potential to produce social resources for learning and change and the potential to be counterproductive to the new goal of "collaboration."

Shifting Politics and Shifting Pedagogy

Mission's staff was struggling with reform during a critical period of transition and ambiguity over education goals—in the MUSD as well as in California. Personal and social conflict in the school interacted with social conflict in the state and district. Staff attempts at melding coherent planning with complex academic standards, already a very difficult task, were complicated by disagreements across the educational system. Thus, a state and district shift toward standardized tests coincided with the federal call for coherence—an irony, given that coherence in the latter case is related to complex performances and high standards. By January 1995, messages from the Goals 2000 initiative, in combination with several other forces, seemed to contribute to a staff shift toward an even narrower school mission—raising CTBS scores in reading—which in turn may have created a school climate less conducive to innovation and the complex instructional reforms for all children.

One important result of the escalating conflict over education in California was the demise of the CLAS, California's short-lived effort at aligning assessment with high intellectual standards of student achievement. The CLAS had run into popular and state-level political resistance, and by the fall of 1994, Louise James reported from Mission Elementary that "the CLAS is dead." The results from the 1993–1994 school year had arrived in February; they were nonexistent for Mission Elementary due to its small sample size. A majority on MUSD's school board had actively opposed most of the assumptions in the CLAS, as did many other school boards in southern California, and they had required that parents formally "opt in" before their child could take the test. Not many did. Another consequence of the contentiousness in the MUSD was that the superintendent resigned in frustration, after much disagreement with her school board, over the reform agenda and other issues. Mather considered the superintendent "a mentor," and "very supportive" of the reform. Now it seemed that support for innovation was evaporating, or at least some confusion temporarily reigned in the MUSD.

Aside from political conflict, new messages from the Goals 2000 initiative and the district office appeared to contribute to the narrower school mission. One important message the school and district leadership received from the planning and application process for Goals 2000 was the importance of clearly articulated goals, based on "student data" and "accountability for results." For example, Mather attended a Goals 2000 grant planning meeting at which California's new state superintendent pressed for a new state focus on "literacy achievement"—more specifically, raising test scores in reading and writing. The Goals 2000 grant criteria Mather received referred often to coherence, clarity, "data-based" decisions, and accountability—all sensible suggestions for school-level and district planning. Mather attended a grant-scoring session for Goals 2000 and reported "all the best grants" had "clearly articulated goals."

Finally, Mather's district supervisor Mark Bills suggested that she use the Goals 2000 grant application process to "restructure" around "the assessment piece." When she returned from the Goals 2000 state meeting, Mather organized a series of school-level assessment and planning meetings to prepare for the Goals 2000 grant process. From those meetings an even narrower mission than the earlier "literacy by the end of first grade" emerged. Now the school mission was "achievement in literacy"—which in effect meant raising CTBS scores in reading.

When asked if Mission Elementary staff saw a connection between Goals 2000 and the reauthorized Title I, Louise James, the Title I coordinator, explained it this way:

> [Goals 2000] is connected [to the Title I program] in that it's a unifying agent . . . it's a way to focus everybody's attention on achievement at this school, because our scores are low and they don't look good up against others. . . . Laura has given this particular chart to teachers—a composite of where all the children are on each track based on CTBS, of where they are by quartile and what their average quartile score was.

One way to account for this further shift toward an even narrower school focus is to consider disagreements across the education system. Federal planners wanted the Title I reauthorization and the Goals 2000 initiative to press toward complex intellectual instruction and curriculum for all students (a move in the direction in which California had been traveling for some time). But the headline policy messages in California began to shift toward a more traditional position of improving basic skills and standardized test results. At least, that is the manner in which they seem to have been interpreted.

For example, at this point in the story, the CLAS no longer mattered the way it had earlier at Mission Elementary. Mission Elementary did not even have student scores. The superintendent and staff who had supported curriculum reforms were gone. Mather's district supervisor appears to have been pressing on standardized test results. And the new state superintendent seems to have been doing likewise—she was interpreted as such after the Goals 2000 meeting. If state and district environments are considered "open systems" (Scott, 1992) that interact with and have at least some influence on schools, all appeared to be moving away, however temporarily, from what the CLAS represented: ambitious instructional reform.

One effect of this general trend was to diminish some of the conflicting messages that were around. Another was to cut short the learning opportunities that staff and leadership at Mission might have had if the CLAS had persisted. While assessments may not "drive" instruction, they can challenge assumptions and provide the "text" for teachers' learning about instructional reform (Cohen & Barnes, 1993a). This had begun at Mission. Louise James was one of more than 2,000 teachers in California who had gathered to examine and score the CLAS statewide. She in turn worked with teachers at Mission to create rubrics based on both the curriculum frameworks and Mission's students' work. This process gave teachers the opportunity to think about specific kinds of student performances in light of a standard aligned with the state frameworks. Such learning opportunities for teachers—when they are focused on content that students study and aligned with assessments—can pay off for students with increased scores (Cohen & Hill, 2001). But concern over learning about or from the CLAS ended when that controversial assessment died.

Another way to account for the shift is to consider the tension between elements of the reforms, between the ideal of school-level coherence and the ideal of complex academic standards. While not necessarily at odds, it is not difficult to see the problems that might emerge in working toward school-wide goal clarity focused on results, and at the same time working toward ambitious curriculum reforms, when the latter in effect requires very complex teacher and student performances. Saying both are important is one matter; putting them into practice is another, because the complexity of "results" in the latter instance is not necessarily a good fit with the technical practices used to assess "results" in the former instance.

For example, the curriculum reforms envision teachers making judgments based on knowledge of curriculum content, their students, and other context-dependent factors. Ambiguity and complexity, not technical clarity, are inherent features of this kind of practice (Lampert, 1985; Little, 1993) for students as well as for teachers. So while Anita Lorenz thought regularly about what would constitute good student work, not only was she ambivalent about what such work would mean in her classroom of diverse children, but her results—demonstrations of conceptual understanding or reasoning skills, for instance—tended to be difficult to capture in school-level or district-level aggregates. Technical advancements in assessments that do capture open-ended reasoning in math or writing samples have lagged behind curriculum development and the reach toward high standards (Cohen, 1995; Little, 1993). For the most part, state and local program managers still rely on standardized tests for measuring "results" and school-level improvement. But standardized tests—while technically sound and suitable for reporting school or district-level student data—embody a view of schooling that can compete with the reforms, as sketched in Chapters 1 and 2. Trying to work coherently toward both kinds of results—ambitious, complex outcomes based on specific curriculum standards, as well as basic skills referenced to national student averages—can be an exercise in coping with contradiction.

Laura Mather and the staff at Mission were coping with this kind of tension, and had to decide what to do when key technical elements in the "systemic reform" puzzle—the CLAS, for example—were missing, in part because of the contentious state and district environment. When pressed to act, and to plan coherently for improvement based on "student data," this school and district responded by using what they had available to them (just as the Chapter 1 Handbook suggested they do). They used CTBS scores.

Striving for clarity centered on school-level results led to a more pronounced focus on a standardized version of student performance. Here coherence at the school level tended to press practices that moved away from, not toward, the complex performances in the curriculum reforms. The schools' decision to press toward clarity—a sharpened, narrower focus and a more coherent school improvement strategy—not only surfaced conflict, but might have also had the unintended consequence of casting success so narrowly, it could shift staff energies away from curriculum reform ideas.

More Conflicts of Meaning

Working interdependently on clear goals was complicated by bilingual goals; and it was made more difficult because teachers disagreed over those goals. For example, Monique Ponds, the Title I bilingual teacher introduced in Chapter 3, worried aloud quite often that Ruth Linn was introducing English "too soon." On this matter she agreed quite strongly with her mentor, the third-grade bilingual teacher Alice Michiels. On the other hand, Juan Ramirez and Ruth Linn, both bilingual teachers, disagreed with the district (and school) policy of "late transition" to English-speaking rooms. Linn especially disagreed quite strongly with the district and school's bilingual policy on the matter of timing.

They both argued that children who speak Spanish ought to be exposed to more English earlier on. They both practiced what they preached, moving from Spanish to English and back in their classrooms. They reported that many of their students were able to speak English (and use it) quite well when they left second grade. But they complained that their efforts were dismantled when third-grade teachers such as Alice Michiels received the students.

Michiels sometimes argued that young Spanish speakers should use only Spanish to learn for conceptual understanding—her master's degree taught her so—therefore, she used mostly Spanish in her classroom. According to district policy, children were to stay in Spanish-speaking classrooms until they were reading and writing at grade level in Spanish (at least at the 75th percentile), using the district's third-grade basal reader test. And they needed to score as a "fluent English speaker" on the English fluency test.

While both Juan Ramirez and Ruth Linn disagreed with the district's bilingual policy, they did so for different reasons. Linn argued that some Spanish-speaking children would never achieve at a level high enough to meet the district standards for transition. She said:

> There are some students who will never meet the district's criteria for transition—they actually have a transition team that you have to go and present your case to—so how many years are you going to [wait]?

But Juan Ramirez reported the bilingual program at Mission allowed, even fostered, standards that were too low for Spanish-speaking kids. According to both Ramirez and Mather, some teachers at Mission did not have high enough expectations for Spanish-speaking students. This belief on the part of Ramirez was one source of the conflict that erupted between the kindergarten teachers and the first-grade teachers over literacy standards.

Success, according to Ramirez, meant students achieving at high levels in at least one language, just as he had in school. But he argued that many bilingual teachers were not prepared to teach to high standards in Spanish, and that the district had no supporting networks once students left Mission Elementary for junior high school. For example, on the first point, he said:

> Take a poll sometime, and find out how many bilingual teachers actually pick up Spanish literature on weekends or just to read for pleasure . . . the percentage would be less than three or two or one percent. . . . Most of the Spanish that the bilingual teachers speak is very superficial. . . . It's not a very proficient language base in Spanish, and yet they're expected to develop some very high-order skills in Spanish. You can't teach poetry if you don't have the language. At the same time, they've got English [to teach]. It's a burnout.

So unlike Ruth Linn's reason for wanting to teach English to her second graders—that is, that they may never perform well enough in any language to qualify for transition to English—Ramirez thought using English sooner would help Spanish-speaking students achieve to higher standards later.

A PERSONAL AND PROFESSIONAL TAKE ON POLICY PRINCIPLES: A FIRST-GENERATION AMERICAN TEACHER

Juan Ramirez's conception of academic standards was informed in part by his life experience and his personal convictions. His parents emigrated from Mexico and he lived for some time in a Los Angeles barrio. He talked about his students and the standards he sets for them in light of his own life:

> Most of my kids, their parents had them when they were fifteen, sixteen. . . . And their level of education is very low. Their expectations for being able to even leave the barrio and make it? They don't think that they really can do it. . . . That really affects the way [students] think. . . . But I do believe [they can make it out] because I'm a case of that. That's why I teach. That's why I don't live in the barrio anymore. Because I believe in myself. . . . They [his students] need to be exposed to somebody who . . . can aspire.

In Ramirez's case, aspiring to high standards of achievement for his students appeared to be a very personal matter. His understanding of his students' experience reinforced his expectations for them and informed his teaching. Collaborating with others around a clear goal might have been a matter of compromising deeply personal convictions bound up in his identity:

> I've lived in a barrio; I understand what it feels like to have to know more than one language in order to survive. . . . I know what it's like to be around drugs and alcohol. . . . I lived in a house with my grandparents, uncles, aunts. . . . That is part of my experience; it's part of me.

But his attitudes also square nicely with the professional norm of holding high academic expectations for all students, and of taking professional responsibility for meeting those expectations. Thus Ramirez was, in some respects, a leader for the reform norms: For personal as well as professional reasons, he was ready to fight for his standard of student achievement and teaching.

Juan Ramirez's family story is one of ambition, self-reliance, and achievement. His grandfather was killed in the Mexican revolution, and Ramirez's parents eventually immigrated to this country from Mexico. By 1960, around the year that Juan Ramirez was born in California, the census documented that Mexican Americans had, on average, 4 years less education than Anglos, as well as a higher unemployment rate. Over 80% of the Mexican American population in America at that time lived in urban areas. Juan Ramirez and his parents were one such family.

Ramirez knew early that he wanted to go to college, despite his father's opposition. He left home, applied for and received loans, participated in a work-study program, and eventually graduated. Ramirez was a music major at a California state university. He later earned a master's degree in bilingual education. He reported studying history as well as the language arts framework when he was earning his master's.

Ramirez also reported watching with dismay during his undergraduate years as "group movements swallowed up" his friends, many of whom lost their scholarships. He said: "[My friends] lost their scholarships because they thought it was much more important to go out and boycott grapes than go to class." Ramirez continued, "You go to college to educate yourself. . . . There [were] many movements out there, but I felt that I could contribute so much more by just working with people and not being dictated to as to how I should act or talk."

Despite his distaste for collective action, Ramirez was quite passionate about improving conditions for "his group" and decided to teach elementary school, in part as an alternative to fomenting revolution. At the time of this study, Ramirez still believed teaching was a powerful force for change:

> I guess that is why I teach. . . . Revolution is romantic; [but] it's only an ideal. . . . When you get down to reality, historically . . . if you want to see progress, in France, in Mexico, and China; it was all born in the universities, the schools. That's where all the minds are and it is a powerful place. . . . I'm a first-generation American. . . . But I don't see the need to carry it on my lapel. . . . There are some people who say I do nothing [for my group]. . . . Well, my philosophy is, I teach. I teach my kids how to be resourceful, how to educate themselves, how to be able to help themselves.

His choice for his students—education—has long been a chosen route to individual opportunity and economic improvement for immigrants and first-generation Americans. But Juan Ramirez seemed to be growing impatient with the gradual pace of change at Mission Elementary. His attraction to a revolutionary solution surfaced in his advice to Laura Mather: Start a new school; show the door to those who disagree with our vision. In other words, overturn the existing system.

Ramirez's passion for teaching aimed at change was a resource for reform at Mission Elementary. The personal resources he brought to the change process—high expectations for his students (most of whom were poor, limited-English speakers) and a sense of responsibility for achieving them—melded nicely with the call for high standards for all students. But Ramirez also weaves his high regard for the teaching profession, and the sense of agency that he derives from it, throughout his personal accounts. Ramirez thought of himself as a professional with both the responsibility and the capacity to teach his students "how to be resourceful, how to educate themselves, how to . . . help themselves." Thus, both personal history and professional obligation account for his views on bilingual education and curriculum reform.

Like Anita Lorenz, Ramirez exuded confidence in his teaching. That is not to argue that these teachers are certain about instructional practices, but to note their conviction that with hard work, their students could perform complex tasks. This conviction is not simply a personal matter; it can be a resource for improving schools. Research suggests that what teachers understand, believe, and expect from their students can have an effect on student achievement.

But even confident, ambitious, knowledgeable teachers cannot do their job alone—especially in this era of curriculum reform, which demands intellectual rigor, content knowledge, knowledge of method, and knowledge of increasingly diverse students. Such teachers working alone would find it difficult to do their job if they could not count on their colleagues to support their goals. This was the situation in which Juan Ramirez found himself when the new plan pressed for mutual accountability among kindergarten, first-, and second-grade teachers, and opened his own as well as the kindergarten teachers' practices to examination.

Here the themes in his life may have added to the difficulty of rigorous collaboration. Ramirez had a strong penchant toward individualism—in overcoming adversity through individual effort, for example, in avoiding groups, for another. Paradoxically, in leaving home and rebelling against his father's wishes, he demonstrated the independence and self-reliance he understood his father to value. From teaching to surfing, he appears to have selected activities that are in great part individualistic—done not by relying on teamwork, but independently. Ramirez is like many other teachers who prefer autonomy in their work over interdependency. Lortie (1975) found that the "recruitment, socialization and system of rewards in teaching fostered . . . orientations toward . . . individualism" (p. 202). Staff interdependency cut against Ramirez's personal preference as well as established teaching norms. Such work did not appear to come easily to this teacher for whom so much was at stake.

Nevertheless, with little guidance or notice from reform documents to support his work, he, along with a few others, began inventing social resources to boost the collective capacity for change at Mission Elementary. Ramirez began taking a much more public leadership role than the private one he was accustomed to having at Mission Elementary.

CONCLUSION

Mission Elementary's story provides a deeper look at the personal and professional nature of conflict and capacity. Coping with conflict in the process of adapting reform ideals to practice can be productive as well as counterproductive. For example, Ruth Linn's sense of efficacy and responsibility for all her students' achievement fell short of what the new school norm would have required of her—that is, to feel obliged with her colleagues for pressing all students toward high academic standards. Here, the conflict embedded in the professional norm of collective accountability may have been productive in challenging Linn's assumption that some students would never attain third-grade literacy skills (had such a norm been fully established at Mission). But with that social resource missing, Linn's personal view, as it conflicted with the views of Ramirez, Ponds, or Lorenz, for example, likely remained counterproductive because the latter three could not count on Linn to support their instructional goals.

While staff interdependency cut against Juan Ramirez's personal preference as well as established teaching norms, he nevertheless found himself among a handful of unlikely leaders of a dramatic change process at Mission Elementary. The decision to restructure brought about a sudden change in relations with his peers: He was placed at the heart of a "joint work" project—working with the kindergarten teachers to see that all students were literate by the end of their first 2 years in school. Ramirez began confronting teachers with whom he passionately disagreed about core teaching issues. Those kinds of issues had long been protected by norms of teaching autonomy (as such issues are protected from debate in most schools).

In this instance, conflict appeared to be productive on two fronts. First, it was a lever for changing Ramirez's autonomous work style. He began taking a public role at the school, a leadership role. Second, by challenging the assumptions of his peers, Ramirez was using personal and professional resources—a strong belief in his students, a sense of efficacy in his instructional capacity, and a passion for teaching aimed at change—to help invent social resources for the school. But he, along with a few others, was trying to create new social relations without much guidance, and without much understanding of the conflict that is perhaps essential to the work of genuine collaboration.

The collective response to Title I and curriculum reforms, as it had thus far been constructed at Mission Elementary, can be interpreted from at least two different angles: (1) conflict and the competition of ideas were counterproductive; or (2) conflict was productive because it helped launch innovation and new, more professional school norms. From the first view, striving for more collaboration and clarity (mutual responsibility for meeting clear agreed-upon goals) surfaced major staff disagreements that led to staff strife—a difficult process that may have worked against the goal of collegiality. Further, the staff move toward clarity appeared to narrow their conception of achievement so as to clash with the complex performances called for in the "high standards" reform. One irony of this reform as it had thus far been constructed at Mission Elementary was that emotionally charged conflict emerged from the process of working toward stronger collegial relations, thus perhaps weakening the social fabric of the school staff, at least temporarily creating a more difficult work environment. It would be another irony of the federal call for "high standards for all children" if in this school, by grafting a school-level, technical coherence on to the nuance and complexity of curriculum reform, standards for Title I students were lowered.

In part, the latter shift at Mission is a reflection of the fragmented system and shifting political environment that the school staff worked within. For instance, the opportunity to learn from the CLAS was no longer there at Mission Elementary when I left that school. And there was talk at the state level of eliminating the just-begun program quality review (PQR) process that asked teachers to collect and talk about student work samples. That process was written about as "an unnecessary burden to schools" (California State Department of Education, 1995). But that is the sort of "untidy," less certain, results-oriented "data" that teachers will likely need to converse over to make sense of the more complex instructional reforms. They will need such processes to critique each other's work and ground their conversations about reform in classroom practices.

On the other hand, from the second view (conflict was productive), the push for more coherence and collaboration challenged existing school norms at Mission Elementary. While the drive for goal clarity and mutual responsibility surfaced conflict, it also opened individual practices to scrutiny, and moved the staff toward norms more conducive to achieving consistent and high academic performances. The staff's deliberation, albeit laced with strong feelings and disagreements, could enhance the level and quality of learning about the meaning of reform in this school. The process has the potential to improve the organizational capacity of the school by creating social resources for change—consistent support for instructional goals, a common understanding, trust, professional accountability, and so on. The process allows teachers with only partial knowledge and understanding to exchange what they know, to create "scaffolding" for one another. The process of inventing these kinds of social resources was under way at Mission, and that process was productive, at least in part.

It seems likely the two views just sketched are interacting contributions to the process of adapting and integrating policy ideals to particular contexts—that is, coping with conflict is integral to the work of putting policies and programs into practice. At Mission Elementary, conflict was related to both productive and counterproductive "fits and starts, and was embedded in the change process—especially in the school-wide reform, but also in many of the dilemmas individual teachers were managing around the demanding reforms.

This key aspect of reform has too often gone without mention in reform documents, and has been too often ignored by program planners. Teachers and administrators alike needed more guidance on the problem of coping with the conflict embedded in change. For example, teachers at Mission needed more opportunities to learn about the pitfalls of moving from the isolation of their classrooms into the arena of public debate and challenge. Rigorous collaboration does not occur naturally in schools where such work is a radical departure from established norms. Mather could have benefited from a mentor—a veteran of school change—to guide the work of channeling conflict into productive conversations, or opportunities for teaching and learning. But instructional resources were missing at Mission and at the MUSD, though Mather and a few teachers were trying to invent them.

Advocates of change could make it "safer" for school administrators and teachers to take the huge risk that changing the work norms in a school requires if the difficulties of such change were made clearer—that is, if change agents understood they were not alone in their ambivalence and contradiction. Most schools that undertake real change face similar obstacles. This is especially so in an era of "site-based" management, where serious consequences—including "takeover" schemes and staff dismissal—accompany the risk of "failure." But too often the ideals of "clear, agreed-upon goals and collaborative work norms" are presented as though they were as easy to enact as a walk in the park. The reform image of "collaboration" has a benign aura about it that leaves the challenges hidden. There is a dilemma here for change advocates, because they have to sell the idea of change to the "targets" and agents of the reform. The message that such change is extremely hard and will cause conflict—that it may be counterproductive at times, even as it leads to improvement—is not an easy sell.

The case of reform at Mission Elementary School over time confirms that it is wise to look deeply into what the oft repeated terms "coherence," "collaboration," and "high standards" actually mean in the context of schools and classrooms. In Chapter 6, I take up the tensions among these reform elements at different levels of activity in more detail with a closer look at Title I students' instruction in year 2.

Managing Trade-Offs: A Closer Look at Gains and Losses

There were trade-offs in the new, more coherent school plan. The manner in which the staff managed those trade-offs amplified to Title I students. Thus, there were losses as well as gains for teachers and students alike. Coherent planning at the school level did not necessarily lead to coherent instruction for some Title I students at the classroom level. In year 2, tensions among reform elements at different levels of activity, as well as the vicissitudes of school life, contributed to a more fragmented, narrower conception of instruction for some Title I students *after* the staff's plan to "restructure" went into effect.

A view into Juan Ramirez's first-grade classroom illustrates some of the benefits his students accrued from the new plan to narrow the school mission and concentrate resources in the lower grades. But the contrasting images of Title I instruction before and after Monique Ponds left Mission Elementary illustrates in more detail the meaning of the losses sustained by the third-grade teachers—Alice Michiels and Kate Jones—and their Title I students. What instructional resources did they lose when Title I resources were eliminated from their classrooms? How did they respond to such losses? In essence, how did these particular teachers manage the trade-offs in the collective response to the reform calling for school-wide coherence?

GAINS FOR TITLE I STUDENTS: RESOURCES AND PRACTICE IN A FIRST-GRADE CLASSROOM

Despite the emotional conflict in which Juan Ramirez was embroiled during the 1994–1995 school year, he reported that the process of working toward agreement on goals was promoting needed critique and communication: "We are at odds now because they are opening up their classroom so that other eyes can see and . . . question what is going on. . . . [But] we're learning how to communicate now. . . . Believe me!" Furthermore, this school year (1994–

1995), as a result of the plan that concentrated resources in the early grades, Mr. Ramirez had the support of two adults—one of them a teacher, one a paraprofessional—in his classroom. Ramirez thought that situation was also a gain for his students and teaching. For example, he said having extra help allowed him to work with smaller groups, "because classroom size is thirty-two. The state of California is overwhelmed. . . . We have excessive groups in the classroom and not enough resources." For Juan Ramirez, Mission's new plan to concentrate resources in the lower grades provided a remedy to this problem that was caused in part by a state recession and limits on property taxes.

The new plan provided Ramirez with a bilingual paraprofessional for 3 hours a day and a bilingual Title I teacher for 2 hours a day. The latter was an especially valuable resource to Ramirez, first because she and Ramirez generally agreed on goals and methods. Second, she was a professional—in the midst of changing careers, just finishing her teacher education coursework—who could develop curriculum and whose instruction Ramirez admired. Juan Ramirez reported: "What I like about [Ms. Lake] is that she is . . . being exposed to a lot of the type of teaching that I'm doing now which is exciting because . . . her philosophy . . . supports mine. So, that's good." Here Ramirez and the Title I bilingual teacher had the ability to create social resources, building on the personal resources they each brought to the classroom. They could support each other's work through mutual goals, agreement on methods, trust, and understanding.

Ramirez was less enthusiastic about his bilingual aide because she did not take much initiative when working with students, and she disagreed with him about goals. He reported: "We [don't] have . . . the same philosophy [about teaching]. My aide . . . is into a phonics only approach to [reading]." Thus, he had to develop lessons for her, generally with a goal of teaching phonics skills to students. The attitudes and knowledge that this paraprofessional brought to Juan Ramirez's first-grade classroom did not so readily translate into social resources for Ramirez. Nevertheless, he reported needing her help and generally asked her to work with small groups of students on basic skills—something he reported she felt more comfortable doing and which he agreed his students needed.

An important point here is the difference in individual resources that these two adults brought and could create in Ramirez's classroom. When asked generally about whether having additional adults in his classroom was helpful, Ramirez talked about such resources in this way:

It all depends . . . [sometimes] adults are just like having [another] child in the classroom. . . . So anytime that I can get a certified person who knows how to work with children . . . who can focus on weaknesses and on developing strengths . . . who has the methods, that's great! . . . That's like having another teacher. . . . It's much more of a professional asset.

In these and earlier comments, we hear that Ramirez valued the professional resources—knowledge, skill, and attitudes—the Title I bilingual teacher brought to his classroom. Such was not equally the case for all adults who had worked with him. There were differences between the "professionals" and the "paraprofessionals."

But teachers at Mission even reported significant differences among the aides that Mission hired. For example, unlike Anita Lorenz, who taught her Title I aide the ways of Writers Workshop and who was enthusiastic about the work her aide was able to do, Ramirez did not find his aide as helpful because the aide resisted his teaching style and took little responsibility for students' learning. In this instance, equivalent financial resources did not necessarily translate into equivalent instructional resources in the two classrooms. In the former case (professional versus paraprofessional), differences in financial resources between the bilingual program that funded "aides" and the Title I program that funded his teacher made a significant difference in instructional resources.

Still, Ramirez made it clear that the help of two adults in his classroom made a difference in what he could do. In essence, the resources Ramirez gained under the new plan were able to reduce the class size for this teacher. His students were able to be part of a much smaller instructional group under the new plan, and receive strategy instruction as well as work cooperatively with peers. Those Ramirez thought needed it were able to have special tutoring under the new plan as well. Thus, he was able to use several of the strategies research suggests help students learn to read—mostly because he had additional resources (see, for example, Slavin, Karweit, & Wasik, 1991).

A Snapshot of Resource Gains in Action

In language arts, where once there were 28 to 32 students for most of the day, now there were three groups of nine or ten. Ramirez created three "heterogeneous" groups which then rotated instructors—from Ramirez to Ms. Lake (the Title I teacher) to Mrs. Hernandez (the bilingual aide)—and kinds of lessons so they all received a mix of instruction. Most of the students, Title I or not, received instruction ranging from reform-oriented "language experience"—for example, discussion for understanding and for explicitly practicing reading strategies, practice in reading aloud or writing for authentic purposes, opportunities to dictate stories to adults and then read them back, and so on—to phonics practice with the bilingual aide. One day Mrs. Hernandez was working with a small group on phonics and the skill of alphabetizing a list of words. Ramirez was working with a group on "writing"; what he called "drawing spring." And Ms. Lake was questioning students about the meaning of words in a poem they had read together (about nine or ten in the groups). After 20 minutes, the groups rotated until each group had been with each adult.

The Classroom Teacher's Instruction

Before Ms. Lake arrived, Ramirez had worked with the entire class to read two poems about spring written in Spanish on a large flip chart. Several children read it orally to the group. Then the entire class gathered around him for a conversation about planting and other themes in the two poems. Ramirez asked them to discuss what "to plant" meant. They discussed what happens during the different seasons and the order of the seasons. Finally, the whole group "brainstormed" ideas about spring after Ramirez asked, "What do you think of when you think of spring?" He wrote all the words the children thought of on the poster paper hanging in front of them. Below are snapshots of what followed this activity:*

Shortly after Ms. Lake walked in, Ramirez picked up a small bell and rang it. The children quickly moved into groups and situated themselves around the room: one group at a table with Ms. Lake, another group at a table with Mrs. Hernandez, and another on the floor circled around Mr. Ramirez. Ramirez told his small group (in Spanish) to think about spring, think about the poem, think about all the words they generated about spring.

> *JR* (in Spanish): We're going to review writing. First we'll center the title "spring." Remember to write "spring" with a capital letter . . . Pablo, you're missing a letter. OK, we're going to illustrate. What does that mean?
> *Boy:* Do a drawing?
> *JR:* Very good, Juan. We're going to draw spring. Then we will write what we drew.
> He gives them suggestions to help them out with their drawings using the words from the list they had generated earlier—leaves, to plant, rain, sun, trunk, air (which can mean "wind" in Spanish), rainbow, grass, roots, flowers, baby animals, fruits, bees, flies, seeds, water, birds singing. Throughout the lesson he encouraged them to add more details to their pictures and to explain their drawings to him while

---

*These conversations were all in Spanish and have been translated into English by Justin Crumbaugh, who is currently a graduate student in Spanish literature.

they worked. For example, he asked a couple of students "What is that?" while pointing to something on the drawing and they answered "little chicken," or "dog." "What is it doing?" They responded. JR asked, "Why?" They responded. Pointing to a figure, he asked Pablo, "Why is that so small?" and Pablo answered, "Because it is very far away." They continue this work until JR says: "OK, turn in the papers. It's time for the next group." He rang the bell again.

(Field note, 3/95)

The Title I Teacher's Instruction

At the same time, Ms. Lake, the Title I bilingual teacher, was working with a group of eight children. They read another poem written on a flip chart titled "La Reina Batata" ("The Queen Batata"). Then they conversed and wrote about it on half sheets of plain cream paper that Ms. Lake had passed to each student.

Ms. Lake is pointing to each child, asking them questions, talking with them about the poem. They are all leaning way up onto the table. Many have their elbows on the table with chins resting on their upturned hands. Some are almost laying on the table. Their eyes are on Ms. Lake or the "large book" in which large letters spell out the words to *La Reina Batata*. Ms. Lake is speaking with a great deal of expression. But very often the children are the ones who are talking.

Ms. Lake asks, "What is the queen of batata like?"

A small boy responds, "She has a crown."

Ms. Lake presses him to think about a word in the poem—threaten. She asks him what it means "to threaten." He responds, but not audibly. Then she asks the group for examples of "threatening." She reminds them how the word is used in the poem. . . . Several children respond to her request: "I'll kill you." "I'll beat you up." "I'll cut you up." "I'll eat you." Ms. Lake asks them all to "make a bad mood face" when they reach the part of the poem where "the chef, in a bad mood . . . threatened" the queen. They read it again aloud and this time the children contort their faces. Then, she asks them to describe what the queen feels like when the chef looked at her and she is "abatada" (a word the author invented). One student says that this means that she's angry. Another says "afraid." Ms. Lake presses them to explain why they think the queen is afraid or angry. They continue the discussion in this manner, then write about the poem on their papers until the bell tinkles once again.

(Field note, 3/95)

The Synergy in Instructional Resources

In both of these short excerpts of small group teaching and learning, the students in Juan Ramirez's class are engaged in making sense of authentic texts—poetry, in these instances—through conversation with a teacher and interaction with peers. The children were given the opportunity to learn from their peers. And Ms. Lake was pressing them to use some of the strategies that good readers use to comprehend text—contextual clues, for example—when the group constructed a likely meaning of the invented word in the poem, or when they discussed the meaning of the word "threaten." She connected the poem to students' experience by having them act out the meaning of threatening, and so on. Children were reading in the sense that they were constructing meaning as well as saying the words orally. Individual children were writing with help from the group discussion. Ramirez was pressing students to use the rules he had taught them about writing, as well as their prior knowledge about spring—connecting the text of the poem to what they knew and expanding both. He also asked them to expand the details of what they understood and to explain their thinking as they drew in preparation for writing. All of these are examples of reform-oriented authentic language experience in students' primary language—Spanish.

In addition to the writing and comprehension work, Mrs. Hernandez was working with a group on more basic skills: recognizing beginning sound-letter correspondence, for example, and putting words into alphabetical order for another. All of this instruction—basic word-decoding, skills instruction, and whole language instruction—integrated the Title I curriculum with the classroom core curriculum. And Title I students were integrated in heterogeneous, cooperative groups in the classroom. A few students received more intensive one-on-one or one-on-two tutoring in reading, also in the classroom.

Ramirez explained his reasons for creating these heterogeneous groups:

> The grouping is mixed so that children who have strengths . . . can . . .
> help kids who . . . have been identified as being Chapter One. Also,
> . . . the work that the Chapter One kids will be doing [is] not all
> remedial. They are exposed to problem solving using context . . . they
> are exposed to a whole language reading atmosphere. . . . Kids get
> stuck in a groove . . . because [they] can't decode a B from a D.
> They're just doing . . . sounds . . . when there is so much more to
> reading. Literacy . . . encompasses everything: semantics, skills,
> syntax, grammar. If you're stuck with just . . . Spot and cat . . . I don't
> see that as real reading.
>
> (JR, 3/95)

Here, Ramirez's reasoning for grouping students includes the idea of coopera-tive learning—an idea rooted in cognitive psychology and sprinkled through-out the reform documents. He wants his students to learn from one another. Title I students' instruction was part of Ramirez's regular classroom curricu-lum. Ramirez used literature as the text for teaching literacy, very much in the direction of the "high standards" curriculum reform. But he also included lessons in skill practice, usually taught by his bilingual aide. Ramirez talked about language arts goals and methods for all his first grade students in sev-eral interviews: "We've read . . . almost every book that you saw on that litera-ture cart. And poetry: Poetry is a mainstay in my classroom for the develop-ment of language."

He also said:

> I'm trying to develop their written discourse. They need to know
> these structures . . . how to write the date, select and write a title. Or,
> that brainstorming that we did on spring? Each kid will choose an item
> of interest and then we'll . . . develop them. For instance, we'll write a
> topic sentence and then we'll write two sentences that will support
> that.

Ramirez wants his students to be able to use language effectively, to under-stand the meaning of literature as well as the mechanics of good writing. His conception of literacy, of what it means to read and write, is consistent with the arguments of advocates of authentic language experiences and those of cognitive research. The former want all students to have authentic reasons to communicate effectively (Goodman & Goodman, 1979). The latter suggests interaction with peers provides students with motivation and "scaffolding" for thinking, reading, and writing (Resnick & Klopfer, 1989).

Moreover, because of the relatively small number of students in each group, Ramirez and Ms. Lake were able to engage each student. All the stu-dents in the small groups—"at risk" students as well as those who were not at risk for failure—were responding to questions. The teachers pressed every child in each group to think. While research on meta-cognitive strategies suggests that students can acquire the thinking strategies to become indepen-dent learners (Porter, 1991), children at risk of failing academically are less likely to possess them. They need guided practice and feedback as they *use* thinking strategies (Garcia & Pearson, 1991) in safe contexts such as the small groups these teachers had created. Brophy (1983) and Good (1979) have each shown that "lower ability" students are not generally given much opportu-nity to respond in whole-class instructional arrangements. Ensuring that every student was actively engaged would have been difficult for Ramirez and Ms. Lake had the groups been much larger (30 students, for example).

Thus, the additional resources in Juan Ramirez's room allowed him and his assistants to use a variety of instructional methods which research and theory on reading achievement suggest have the potential to prevent later reading difficulties in students who are at risk for academic failure (Slavin, Karweit, & Wasik, 1991). Ramirez and his students gained from the new plan to concentrate resources and forge mutual staff obligation for a narrower, more focused school mission. But that was not necessarily the case in the third-grade classrooms of Alice Michiels and Kate Jones.

LOSSES FOR THIRD GRADE TITLE I STUDENTS AND TEACHERS

Michiels and Jones had to cope with the tension between the ideal of coherent planning at the school level and the practical problems in their classrooms. When the school's modest human resources were concentrated in the lower grades, Monique Ponds—the Title I bilingual teacher who had been working with the third-grade students 3 days each week—was slated to work in kindergarten through second grade. Ponds would have no longer been available to work with these third-grade teachers.

Michiels's first response to the new plan under which she would lose Monique Ponds was to find a way to keep her. Using flexible funding under new categorical rules, she devised a way for Ponds to stay with the Title I children who had passed from second to third grade. Michiels and a fourth-grade teacher responded creatively to their loss of Title I resources (a "credentialed" Title I teacher in their room an hour a day, 3 days a week) by using bilingual funds—funds that generally were used to hire bilingual aides for several hours a day. They pooled their money to pay for Ponds. By sharing human resources they tried to maintain the continuity in Title I instruction to meet the needs of their students.

But the bilingual funding was less than Title I funding, and it was bound up in a hiring process that made it difficult to find and keep qualified people. So this was not a substitution of one pool of funds for another in several respects. Ponds worked less than the two bilingual aides she was replacing would have worked (aides worked 3 hours each). Furthermore, the substitution of Ponds for a bilingual aide was not something these teachers could replicate. This was a special case because Ponds was willing to work fewer hours for less money: first because she had a new baby; and second because Michiels was her mentor; Ponds wanted to work with her. Still, the teachers thought less time with Ponds was a lucky break for them—a better resource than more time with bilingual aides.

Alice Michiels explained the situation as a human resource problem caused in part by bureaucratic routines and rules associated with the bilin-

gual program. Teachers didn't have any choice over which bilingual aide was
assigned to their class and the district based their hiring on seniority, not on
qualifications. Thus, part of the problem with losing Title I resources and
replacing them with bilingual funds was qualified help: Michiels reported that
she had to train and work with four bilingual aides the previous year. If they
were good, they left for more pay. If they were not, they were more trouble
than the time it took to train them. Thus, fewer funds embedded in a hiring
system that wasn't working well meant that to replace Ponds, Michiels would
have had to select from a pool of bilingual aides who, because of hiring practices, weren't very good.

Despite the third-grade teachers' creative efforts, midway in the school
year, Monique Ponds quit because she was not able to net enough money to
make ends meet due to the high cost of child care. This situation is another
example of the practical considerations—budget constraints and the lack of
qualified help—that can conflict with staff attempts at coherent planning.
Another is the transient student population. Monique Ponds left in her wake
several Title I students who appeared to be struggling to "make it" in the
regular classroom, but who now had no help because of the new, more coherent school-level plan. One of those students transferred in from another
school, and according to three reports, was suspected of having been a "crack
baby." There were trade-offs in the choices Mission's staff had made—losses
as well as gains. And teachers had to cope with those trade-offs.

Before and After Losing Resources

Contrasting images of Title I instruction—before and after Ponds's departure
from Mission—illustrate in more detail the tension that can occur among reform elements—the call for school-wide coherent planning and the press for
more coherent, demanding instruction for Title I children, for example—at
different levels of activity. The fact that practical conflicts with the policy
ideals (such as those described above) occur is a theme that appears repeatedly in this study. But here, a closer look at the school shows the meaning
these conflicts hold for teachers and students, and how teachers at Mission
coped with them.

Bilingual, Title I Instruction Before the Resource Loss

At the beginning of the 1994-1995 school year—before the school's mission
had narrowed to raising CTBS scores, but after the plan to concentrate resources in the lower grades—the literacy activities in Michiels's room (as in
Lorenz's and Ramirez's) were, for the most part, consistent with California's
English-language arts model curriculum. For example, the curriculum guide

(California State Department of Education, 1987, 1988) suggests that teachers use authentic texts and that all students actively engage with such texts: "Beginning in the primary grades the instructional materials used for the English-language arts program should be oriented less toward textbooks . . . and based more on literature" (pp. 2–3). And: "Students [should] have ample opportunities to discuss, listen, read, write, and also to experience literature in a setting which fosters active and not merely passive participation" (p. 2).

Before Monique Ponds's departure, she and Alice Michiels worked to integrate this kind of literacy reform with Title I instruction in Michiels's classroom. Their expectations for Title I students were in definite contrast to traditional expectations for such students at the time of this study—expectations that included a heavy emphasis on "basic" component skills apart from classmates, meaningful texts, or genuine purposes for academic tasks. Michiels stressed that though Ponds pulled aside some students for special tutoring, she did so during "nonacademic" times, such as the morning opening, or to support their work on assignments that the entire class was doing. Both Ponds and Michiels reported that the Title I instruction was aligned with the regular classroom instruction, and observations seemed to confirm their reports.

In one reform-oriented literacy lesson, the two teachers had planned to integrate reading and speaking for authentic purposes, for the students. For example, the class had selected a poem and read it to their parents as part of their homework. Five Title I children were working on pictures that illustrated each of the poem's verses in preparation for an oral presentation to the entire class. While doing so, they were having a running conversation with Ponds about words in the poem, the meaning of the poem, and their drawings. Ponds frequently helped students with a variety of mechanical tasks, and with "sounding out" words. She also pressed them to think about their illustrations. Here they began by talking about how an ostrich might look like a ballerina in a skirt—an image used in a verse about ostriches:

> *MP:* How do ballerina dresses appear, do you imagine? Have you all
> seen a ballerina?
> They all respond enthusiastically that yes, they have. One child says
> that he saw a practicing ballerina in Mexico and describes her to the
> group. She carried paper streamers in her hand. After a bit more
> discussion in which students describe ballerina skirts they resume
> work on their illustrations.
> *MP* (to another child): What else can you do for this scene? Where do
> tigers live? Can you think? In mountains? In trees? (This was a
> reference to information the children had covered in science
> yesterday, but it was also an image in the poem.)

> *Child:* Among trees? (They continued for a while, then at one point, Nan read her verse aloud spontaneously. Ponds said she was preparing for the big moment in front of the class. Ponds turned to Ana.)
>
> *MP:* Ana? Honey? I want you to do more with your drawing. (There was a pause; then Ana said)
>
> *A:* Uh-huh (nodding affirmatively).

These examples are instances of Title I students being pressed to think about and respond to images in poetry through images of their own. Ponds not only keeps them on task, but pushes them to expand their work, eliciting "background knowledge" from previous reading or experience. This instructional episode also seems to illustrate the "internal motivation" that researchers argue can be generated through authentic tasks. Several students were reading the verses they had copied below their illustrations, not because the teacher had asked them to do it, but because they wanted to prepare for the class presentation. This sort of oral reading is in contrast to what has been reported as more typical—that is, small groups of students in "read arounds" reading aloud from basals, repeating the same paragraphs while others follow along (Knapp & Shields, 1991). This day, according to Ponds, the children in her group were eager to rehearse their verses aloud by reading or reciting—outside as well as in the classroom.

At 9:35 a.m., Alice Michiels tested the microphone—"testing, one, two"—then introduced Ponds and her students. They were gathered in front of the room holding their pictures. Ponds began in Spanish:

> *MP* (Spanish): My group chose a poem about the zoo, and each person . . . is going to recite [a verse] to you. . . . The poem is called "the zoo." Ana? (After a pause, Ana began reading the verse "the tigers" in Spanish, into the microphone. Her usually quiet, almost inaudible voice carried throughout the room as she spoke.)
>
> *Ana* (Spanish): the striped tigers. (pause.) The striped tigers are lying down because they feel sl . . . sl . . . sleepy.
>
> *MP:* very good. (applause from the entire class)
>
> Then Nan stood in front of the group to recite her verse. She had it nearly memorized and spoke into the microphone with gusto, all the while holding her illustration up for the others to see.
>
> *Nan* (Spanish): The polar bears. White polar bears like the foam, like the clouds, dreaming snow.
>
> (More applause and Maria began.) She also held her poster up to the group. Everyone in the room appeared to be attending to the presentation. Maria had drawn a picture of dancing ostriches.

She read the following: "The ostriches. Dressed in their feathers, the ostriches (pause) look like ballerinas (pause) waiting for them to turn on the lights."

(Field note and audiotape, 8/94)

When Ponds's group of students finished to great applause, Michiels had several other students read or recite to the class over the microphone. Michiels and Ponds's goal over the course of the week was to have all of the children make a public presentation to an "authentic audience," one they cared about. All presentations were made in Spanish. According to Ponds and Michiels, Ana (the tiny girl who had been born prematurely in the outback of Mexico) managed to exercise her oral language skills, boost her confidence, practice reading, as well as "experience and respond to" literature—all while practicing the mechanics of language. Though Ana had far to go, Ponds believed that she was making headway: the previous year she could not read; now she was beginning.

The images from Michiels's classroom square with "alternatives to conventional wisdom" (Knapp & Shields, 1991) in the literacy curriculum reforms—specifically with the California curriculum guide that wants students to learn the mechanics of reading and writing through an integrated language approach. Such an approach has them actively engage with literature, cooperatively, in interaction with peers. Her instructional goals were also consistent with Title I reforms that want Title I students to have access to the "core curriculum," and want instruction coordinated with, rather than fragmented from, "regular" classroom instruction.

When Michiels lost Ponds, she lost a valuable human resource: a dedicated teacher who held beliefs similar to Michiels about teaching as well as bilingual policy; a professional who was capable of designing curriculum and instruction; and a supportive colleague who was helping Michiels integrate Title I instruction into the regular reform-oriented, classroom curriculum (in language arts). Kate Jones also lost an important resource—a trained and conscientious tutor she could rely on to work with students who needed extra help.

English, Title I Instruction Before the Resource Loss

What Jones *had* in the vignette below, but then *lost*, due in great part to the new plan to concentrate resources, was an important human resource. When Kate Jones lost Ponds, she lost a tutor for a handful of students who seemed desperately to need it, in part because transient students made long-range planning difficult in this school. For example, the new plan assumed students would be "readers" when they reached third grade. But in this example, Kyle,

the boy who left Anita Lorenz's second grade class as a "reader," was no longer
at Mission. (Though Gerard was, and he was one of Ponds's students.) Diane,
the Title I student who took Kyle's place, transferred into Kate Jones's room
from another school.

What follows is an excerpt of a lesson with Diane, a girl whom both Kate
Jones and Monique Ponds reported was a "nonreader." The day of this lesson, Ponds reported they would read from a Dr. Suess book—*Great Day for
UP*. The previous day, Jones had wanted Diane to "do phonics" and Diane
"hated it." So Ponds promised Diane she could read a book that day. But Ponds
read the entire story to Diane, sometimes stopping to talk about what words
or phrases might mean and to find clues in the pictures; sometimes stopping
to coach Diane on the one word she was able to read—UP.

> Diane, a little black girl, walked up to the table. Ponds asked Diane,
> "Have you ever read this book before?" Diane shook her head no.
> "Have you read any Dr. Suess books before?" Again, D shook her head.
> "Do you know what rhyming words are?" she asked.
> Diane said: wake-up, wake-up.
> *MP* (looking puzzled): Well, those words are repeating words.
>   Rhyming words would be like Jake baked a cake. Let's see if this
>   book rhymes. [She opens the Dr. Suess book.] . . . The only word
>   that you're going to have to read in this whole book is this word
>   [she points to, but does not read, the word UP written in bold red
>   letters on the cover of the book: *Great Day for UP*]. Can you
>   read it?
> *D:* wake up
> *MP* [still looking puzzled]: Not quite. Now how did you think of
>   saying wake up? Why are you saying wake up, wake up?
> *D:* I just looked at the book.
> *MP:* Well this says up [pointing to UP] and the book has to do with
>   waking up. You're right! I'm impressed with how you noticed
>   that. Okay, the title is *Great Day for UP*. So the one word you're
>   going to read every time you see it is this word here . . . [pointing
>   to UP!]
> *D:* wake
> *MP:* not wake the other one you said. Uuuuuuuuh?
> *D:* up
> *MP:* up. So why don't you start. I'm going to point to the word [Ponds
>   points to the first two words UP! UP!]
> *D:* up (long pause) up
> *MP:* the sun is getting
> *D:* up

MP: Good. The sun gets?

D: up

They continue for a few moments, then

MP: Ear number one. Ear number two. See how this sort of rhymes?
The sun gets up. So up with YOU . . . [she points to the next UP
and says] "Here's your word."

Diane pauses for a while, then purses her lips to make a "W" sound.
Then she says, "wake-up."

MP: Up

D: Up . . .

MP: heads

D: Up

MP: whiskers, tails! Great day, today. Great day forrrrrr?

D: waaa, wu, waaake

MP: Look at those two letters. Just two letters. Uhhhhh [Ponds made
the short u sound with her mouth and finally D said the word]

D: Up.

They continued with Ponds reading and pausing for Diane to read UP.
Then they talked about a picture for a few moments and Ponds asked
Diane some questions which she seemed to readily and sensibly
answer. After a while Ponds read: great day to sing up on a wire.
Diane immediately noticed that Ponds had read the word UP.

Diane said: you said I could read UP

Ponds responded: Oh, you know, you're right. Let's start over.

MP: great day to sing . . . (pause)

Diane pressed her lips together and said: my. mmmmmm.

Ponds said: Uhhh uhhh

D: UP!

They finished the story in this manner. Diane read "her word" several
more times. Then near the very end at the word "up," Diane said,
"wake."

Ponds pointed in the book and said, "This one is wake. What is
this one [up]. The one you've been saying. Everyone on earth is . . . ?
Don't you remember? The u and the p? Uuuhhhh?"

D: uuuhhh

Ms. Ponds: UP

D: UP.

(Field note and transcript, 8/94)

All of Kate Jones's students were choosing, reading, and responding to Dr.
Suess books from the library this week. The excerpt above shows that several of these students were struggling, very much in need of the extra tutor-

ing. Ponds was only with Michiels and Jones for a few months because of their special arrangement, and they could not replace her when she left. Thus, the vignettes not only illustrate the resources these teachers' students had—before the new plan went into effect and before Monique Ponds left the special situation of their employment—but also what the upper-grade teachers lost under the new plan.

Managing Tensions After the Loss of Resources

The situation also illustrates the tension between coherent school-level planning and coherent planning for instruction at the classroom level. Likewise, it shows how long-range planning is in tension with the practical problem of a highly transient student population. Michiels had been in favor of the new school-level plan the previous spring. She, along with her colleagues, developed the plan with a school-wide goal in mind. Michiels reported:

> I thought [the plan to concentrate resources and focus on the early grades] was a great idea. Because . . . if we helped these students earlier, we may not be seeing the type of needs [we have] now. That was the main reason. Let's do prevention; let's try—we've tried remedial, that doesn't work. . . . Let's try prevention.
> (AM reporting on the previous spring, 6/95)

But after the plan went into effect Michiels spoke for other upper-grade teachers when asked how it had worked over the course of the year:

> Well, it just kind of left us in a lurch for those kids that were struggling. . . . So we have had to come up with other ideas for working with those kids. . . . Teachers weren't happy with the new plan because they have some kids that are nonreaders. I had a lot of students that were not reading. So I . . . relied heavily on the [new peer] tutoring program to increase their fluency, and it has worked with some of them. . . . So [we coped] by restructuring . . . and doing some pull-outs, but with [fifth-grade] students—having them teach each other—rather than relying on the Chapter One teacher who wasn't going to be there for us.
> (AM, 6/95)

Here Michiels's comments express concerns about the instruction of particular students. Teaching is interpersonal. Individual students, with whom teachers have personal relationships, influence their sense of efficacy. With limited financial resources and a transient student body, they were coping with the tension between what was best for the school and what was best for their particular students.

There were several reports from third- and fourth-grade teachers about situations similar to the one Kate Jones and Alice Michiels were facing: students who could not read a word were transferring into their classrooms. The upper-grade teachers coped with the consequences of the new, more coherent school-level plan, as Alice Michiels noted above, by relying on multiple "pull-outs" for Title I students—a situation that likely produced less coherent instruction for those students.

By midyear, Ponds was gone and her students were pulled out for a drill-oriented peer tutoring program during which fifth-grade students were tutors. All the students I was following went to peer tutoring, two others went to RSP (the special education resource specialist program), and one went back to second grade. In all, 12 students left Michiels's room and she reported this gave her the relief she needed to then work with the 20 students who were left in the room during writers workshop. Kate Jones also reported sending students to special education.

Gerard, who had worked so hard last year in Anita Lorenz's class to make it out of RSP into the regular classroom, was back in special education. He was "pulled out" of Jones's classroom to receive instruction from the resource specialist. Gerard had lost not only his natural mother, who was in jail pending a trial for murder, but the "home to school bridge" Monique Ponds had created for him—that is, a personal relationship serving as an important thread of continuity in his life (Comer, 1986, 1990; Delpit, 1986, 1988). Gerard was also in the special new "peer tutoring" program, as were Maria, Nan, and most others in the two small groups of Title I students. Ana—the tiny girl Ponds had pushed to stay on task and to recite poetry to her classmates over a public announcement system—now received much of her instruction away from her classmates, in the special education room. Diane, the girl who had difficulty remembering the word UP, had been sent back to second grade.

The literature on retention suggests that generally such a remedy has no long-term benefits for individual children (Slavin & Madden, 1991). And retention in the early grades is a major predictor of school dropout (Lloyd, 1978). Some researchers have been critical of retention as well as the practice of shifting students to special education programs—using labels such as "learning disabled," "language impaired," or "emotionally disturbed"—arguing there is little evidence that such practices have positive effects on students (Mehan, Hertweck & Meihls, 1986). Some suggest there have been incentives for Title I schools to use these practices to "raise" their test scores by eliminating the lowest scores (McGill-Franzen & Allington, 1991; Slavin & Madden, 1991). But in this instance at Mission Elementary, placing Diane in second grade (where there were three adults working in the classroom) rather than leaving her in

Kate Jones's room without help, is one way to manage a dilemma: choosing between school-level coherence or instructional coherence for particular children when resources are limited. Sending Ana and Gerard to special education services is yet another way to cope with a loss of resources and the students' academic struggles.

With only modest resources in this school of 950 students, there were trade-offs in the staff's school-wide choices. In part, the "solution" to one problem created another one. The staff's response to the new problematic situation was not unreasonable, especially from their perspective, but it may have contributed to the ironic turn at Mission away from the policy ideal of high curriculum standards for all children toward a more fragmented curriculum and narrower conception of achievement for some Title I students.

Title I Instruction After the Loss of Resources

For example, Catherine Crosby, the special education teacher who initiated peer tutoring at Mission, demonstrated the program for two groups of prospective fifth-grade tutors and their teachers:

> 9 a.m.: In front of a group of students, a third grader [Maria, Ponds's former student from Alice Michiels's classroom] reads a short segment of text from an overhead projection, in Spanish. She is timed by a fifth grader while doing so.
>
> Catherine Crosby asks the entire group, "How many mistakes did she make?"
>
> Students in chorus say: "One!"
>
> Crosby says, "Show how the mistakes are recorded." A fifth-grade tutor points to the zeros on the overhead, signifying a mistake in the segment of text the third grader has read. The two girls demonstrate a timed reading [for the second time]. The mistakes are pointed out, corrected, and the passage is read again—four times in all.
>
> Crosby gives examples of problems that tutors bring up—for example, "How can I keep my tutee's finger on the words?"
>
> During another demonstration, Maria reads a list of vocabulary words, one of them incorrectly.
>
> Her fifth-grade tutor Pat points to the word and says (in Spanish), "This word is stone."
>
> Maria repeats the word "stone."
>
> The older girl continues reading vocabulary words and the younger one repeats them after her. . . . Now Pat reads a segment of text projected by the overhead onto the screen. Then Maria reads, repeating what the older girl had read. All the while the two girls are

using a pen and finger to point out errors and follow the text on the overhead projector. Maria's small finger moves from word to word as she reads; Pat's pen does the same.

Crosby explained that this routine is used so that they don't get lost. Then she explained that this is timed reading and that the tutor reads the passage once and the tutee reads it three times. They set a time of one minute to see how much the tutee can read in that time; and the tutor records the errors.

(Field notes and audiotapes, 6/95)

The vignette shows a drill and practice approach to reading using repeated, rapid, timed readings of a segment of text or vocabulary words. At this point in the story, for some of Mission's second- and third-grade Title I students, "improvement in achievement" was conceptualized as increasing the speed and accuracy of reading sight words or pieces of text. And "student data" meant charting the errors in a segment of text after drilling students on it. Crosby's description of peer tutoring squared with the call for accountability. According to an explication of the tutoring model Crosby was using, the student readers' "progress toward specific objectives . . . [is] . . . measured daily" (Jenkins & Jenkins, 1987). And peer tutoring lent itself to technical transfer of program practices because students could be trained to replicate them. But as I argued in Chapter 5, while the program methods may be transferable and "effective," the aims do not represent high standards, nor do they call for complex performances on the part of teacher or student.

Further, these students were pulled out of their regular classroom to receive this instruction, as well as special education instruction. In all these ways, instruction for some Title I students moved closer to the inherited images of fragmented pull-outs with a focus on "low-level" skills, an image that the various reforms—both Title I and curriculum reforms—had been aiming to change. Whether these students needed this kind of instruction is a matter of debate. Research is very divided on what is most effective for disadvantaged children. But, from the point of view of the reforms and based on at least some research, this move represented a loss for this group of Title I students. At Mission Elementary, coherence at the school level did not necessarily translate into coherence at the instructional level.

CONCLUSION

The fate of reform at Mission Elementary depended in part on the staff's capacity to manage or cope with conflict, and at the same time transform traditional "inputs" into productive instructional resources. The staff made difficult choices about their school mission and how to use their limited resources. Thus, as with any such decision where people set priorities and make choices using limited financial resources, there were gains as well as losses for teachers and students. Juan Ramirez and his first-grade students gained from the all-staff decision to concentrate resources in the lower grades and forge mutual staff obligation for a more specified school mission—literacy for all students by the end of first grade. But that was not the case for Alice Michiels, Kate Jones, and at least some of their third-grade Title I students. Mission Elementary school's staff had to cope with trade-offs between reform ideals at different levels of activity—coherence at the school level or coherence for individual students at the instructional level.

But the instructional resources—gained and lost under the new, more coherent school plan—depended in part on personal or professional resources that individuals brought to the tasks of teaching children, and on social resources created by staff at the school. Thus equivalent funding did not always translate into equivalent instructional resources. Rather, individual or collective knowledge, belief, skill, motivation, expectations for student work, and so on, shaped in part the extent to which financial resources could be transformed into valuable instructional resources in classrooms. In some instances similar levels of funding (only somewhat less or more) translated into dramatically different instructional resources, depending on factors such as hiring practices and qualified personnel— for example, in the case of bilingual funding versus Title I funding.

In other instances, as in the case of paraprofessionals in Ramirez's classroom and Lorenz's classroom, differences were less dramatic but nevertheless important for instruction. Anita Lorenz was able to create social resources—trust, mutually reinforcing goals, complementary instruction—with her paraprofessional who was eager to learn and who held the same high expectations for students' work as Lorenz did. Thus, Lorenz was able to transform the funding she received for a Title I aide into a key instructional resource for her students. For the same amount of funding, Ramirez received neither the social resources nor the key instructional support that Lorenz did, in part because of the attitudes and knowledge his paraprofessional brought to the classroom. However, Ramirez and his Title I teacher were able to build on the personal and professional resources they brought to support each other's instruction: they sent consistent messages to students because of mutual aims and means, understanding, trust, and so on. Social resources for reform resided in their relationship.

Thus conventional resources—funding and staffing allocation—did not necessarily affect the capacity for instructional improvement directly. Personal resources were not "widgets" that were easily produced or evenly distributed. Similarly, the trust, understanding, and mutual expectations that resided in relationships created by the staff at Mission could be quite powerful resources. But they, too, were not necessarily interchangeable, and they took time to create. Still, there were clearly gains and losses in the new school-wide plan. The increased number of adults *did* make a positive difference for Juan Ramirez and his students. And the upper-grade teachers lost the time and energy of a capable, dedicated professional when they lost Monique Ponds—a teacher who held high expectations for students, someone they could rely on to work with students who needed extra help. Alice Michiels especially lost a supportive colleague whom she had taught and with whom she had spent hours talking about teaching.

Likewise, the students who lost Monique Ponds as their tutor lost not just a teacher, but a personal relationship that had been building for over a year. For children who are struggling to live their lives as well as learn to high standards, such a loss is significant. The academic problems these children faced were an important target of the curriculum and Title I reforms. But the social and academic problems the students brought to the task of enacting the reforms—that is, of learning to high standards—inhibited their capacity for strong performances. Without the added value of Monique Ponds's personal and social resources, many of her students will no doubt flounder.

The upper-grade teachers were torn between what was best for the school and many of its students in the long run—preventing reading problems, thus avoiding later remedial work—and the immediate needs of particular students who were struggling—students with whom they had personal relationships. When professional efficacy depends in part upon the personal relationships between individual students and their teachers, watching even a handful of students flounder and fail is difficult. These teachers managed by reverting to a drill and practice pull-out strategy, special education pull-outs and, in the case of one child, retention, thus taking an ironic turn away from the 1988 Title I Hawkins-Stafford reform amendments to which they had earlier responded so ambitiously. Though our view of policy implementation and reform ends here, at Mission Elementary, and in similar schools across America, the story no doubt continues.

CHAPTER 7

The Fate of Education Reform: Problems and Possibilities

In this book I set out to examine the dilemmas that American educators and reformers face in light of the situated action in one school. Mission Elementary and the work of the staff there represent a microcosm of key issues in American education today: first because of their situation—the school enrolled many poor, language-minority, immigrant children; next, because for the most part the staff was trying hard to enact a set of difficult reforms, unprecedented in recent history, calling for intellectually rigorous instruction for all children, rigorous professional collaboration, and coherent planning. Finally, Mission represents current issues in education because of the contentious political environment surrounding and infusing the staff's work. The competition of ideas in California was fierce, but not uncommon for American education. Thus, the school was not only a fascinating study, but also a difficult and rewarding place for its faculty and students.

Understanding curriculum reform has meant looking deeply into what highly touted and hopeful solutions to the problem of low achievement among poor minority students actually mean in the context of schools—solutions such as "clear, agreed-upon goals" and "collaboration," or "school-wide coherence," "school restructuring," and "high standards." The staff at Mission Elementary had, for the most part, embraced the complexity of "high standards for all children"—that is, curriculum reforms—and was wrestling with the issue in a somewhat intellectually incoherent school climate, where teacher autonomy was the reigning norm. They had also worked for years to organize instruction in ways that were responsive to the 1988 amendments to Title I, calling for less fragmented instruction for Title I students.

Then the staff embarked on another project: school-level coherence; that is, trying to "restructure" their work norms toward more interdependence and to be clearer about their mutual goals in light of measurable results. A growing body of research tells us such social relations and technical alignment between aims and means can make schools more effective, improve student achievement. But given the mismatch between their resources and the difficulty of the task; competing messages from federal, state, and district sources; and a political shift in California toward standardized testing, this second wave of Mission Elementary's response to reform, though potentially productive, also seems ironic in that it may have moved some instruction and staff energy away from the goal of high standards for all students. By embracing one aspect of the reforms through coherent planning, the school moved away (in some classrooms) from another aspect of the same reforms—that is, integrating Title I students with their peers rather than separating them through pull-out programs stressing basic skills.

That is not to argue that enacting reforms at Mission Elementary was a zero-sum game in which losses negated gains. But the summary of Mission's response to reforms over time provides just one example of how this staff had to cope with tensions in the reform ideals as they worked to merge them in practice.

Variations on that central theme—coping with conflict with only modest resources—was a key pattern that emerged as educators at Mission Elementary worked to adapt policy and program ideals to the context of their school. Those variations ranged from the internal conflict or dilemmas with which individuals were coping, to the overt, social, and sometimes very emotional disagreements with which the staff had to cope, to the dilemmas or tensions the staff shared as a group. Managing the dilemmas in American education is not at all like solving a problem, once and for all. It involves ongoing work, even struggle. Mission's staff was struggling with the serious health and welfare problems their children faced in addition to transforming their teaching and school organization. They were doing so with inadequate social or professional resources for the task before them. And they also lacked the technical resources they needed (e.g., a technically defensible and politically feasible assessment aimed at complex intellectual achievement).

Because these problems that educators at Mission were facing are not "tidy" and "solvable" (Cuban, 1984), Mission's response to the reforms was regularly changing as educators there learned from experience: It has no doubt carried on. Given the historical context sketched in Chapter 1, this is not surprising. The problem of low achievement among poor, minority, limited-English-speaking children, like many social problems, has long been under attack by educators and social scientists alike, and it has had a shifting definition. The "problem" has become more complex, and potential "remedies" perhaps more contradictory as a result of social scientists' divergent attempts at understanding them over the years (see, for example, Lindblom & Cohen, 1979, or Marris & Rein, 1982).

The current reforms envision both complex thinking performances for all students and mastery of basic skills; coherent, research-based, "results"-oriented strategies and high intellectual standards of achievement; clear, focused goals and staff collaboration—which perhaps does not require consensus, but is made more difficult without it. Those ambitious policy ideas are coming from a system in which social scientists, politicians, and policy planners disagree and in which popular opinion is very divided. At Mission Elementary, the disagreements Americans have had over education were embodied and interpreted by yet another group of actors, with their own particular histories shaping their response to the ideas. Thus, another layer of competing commitments and conflicts in meaning emerged as Mission's staff mediated program or policy ideas.

THE INTERPLAY OF CONFLICT AND CAPACITY

Thus, the fate of the curriculum standards reform at Mission Elementary depended on what the enactors understood and were able to do in the midst of conflict and inconsistency. Conflicting policy purposes; conflicting professional commitments; social conflict; and conventional, social, or personal resources interacted to shape enactors' capacity to understand and adopt complex instructional reforms. Gains as well as losses emerged from the process for students and teachers alike. But generally, when capacity or capacity-building resources were lacking—because of inherited ideas about teaching or work norms, too few serious learning opportunities, incomplete prior knowledge, or experience that clashed with reform—then conflict was often counterproductive. For example, because teacher preference was the inherited norm for organizing professional development, conflict in the form of competing priorities diluted the staff's use of reform-oriented professional development funding. Because staff and leadership neither brought the experience for the rigors of serious organizational restructuring nor had opportunities to learn about creating new norms, conflict undermined the social resources the staff was trying to develop (for example, agreement on instructional goals, trust, or joint work accompanied by support as well as challenge). Conflict was also counterproductive for fledgling change attempts by individual teachers, as in the instance of Alice Michiels, in part because of partial knowledge and lack of authoritative support for learning.

When capacity was present—either through prior understanding or conviction (congruent with reform), through learning opportunities found or invented, or through relationships created at the school—conflict could be a productive change mechanism, as in the case of Kate Jones, for example. It could be a stimulus for innovative practices, as in the case of Monique Ponds or Anita Lorenz. Conflict was a productive influence in the instance of Juan Ramirez because it turned his preferred working style from private toward public—that is, he became a leader for reform. Below I take up these examples of conflict at Mission Elementary in more detail in order to examine the process by which conflict and resources—conventional or otherwise—shaped enactors' capacity to respond to reform. The implementation process both required and generated organizational or professional capacity.

Coping with Internal Conflict

Monique Ponds and Anita Lorenz were able to turn competing commitments into productive, innovative practices, due in large part to instructional capacity—the personal or professional resources they brought with them and the social resources they created while on the job. Ponds and Lorenz were two among several teachers trying to manage dilemmas at Mission Elementary. While multiple policies and contradictory program goals contributed to their ambivalence, competing needs were also embodied in their students, and the confounding factors of their variable SES or English-language ability.

Still they were both able to adapt reform-oriented curriculum to the needs of individual students. For example, Anita Lorenz invented an ambitious practice, balancing ideas and commitments in the flux of classroom interaction: such as, in her case, balancing whole language and phonics instruction. And she balanced a commitment to high curriculum standards with her fierce determination to respond to the individual differences in her students. This she did with students ranging from those for whom writing meant "telling" and reading meant "listening" to those who could write a several-page story, and read silently as well as orally with fluency. Lorenz and others like her, such as Monique Ponds, were also ambivalent about another set of contraries—that is, pushing their students hard toward difficult academic standards while at the same time wanting to nurture these small children who were living very difficult lives.

How did these teachers manage to teach in the direction of the complex reforms? Despite the conflict, both Ponds and Lorenz were effective "users" of available resources, due in part to the energy and time they were willing to spend. Lorenz, for example, aggressively recruited resources to her classroom mission—parents, tutors, and so on. They both sought out mentors, people at Mission and elsewhere, with whom they talked frequently about their teaching. Both Ponds and Lorenz were comfortable with the notion of learning while on the job. Both were aggressive about using opportunities (or creating them) to ensure they would continue to do so. They both initiated interdependent work projects with colleagues, observed other teachers, talked about goals, were willing to assume responsibility for mutual goals, and so on.

Ponds and Lorenz both brought considerable personal resources to the task of reform, in addition to the enormous reserves of time and energy noted above. Lorenz reported attending a challenging teacher education program in which she learned to teach in the way of reforms through an "apprentice-ship of observation"—a context in which she was both challenged and sup-ported by mentors, instructors, and peers. She left that program willing to embrace uncertainty. Thus, Lorenz brought a willingness to "maintain con-tradictory positions while acting with integrity" (Lampert, 1985, p. 183) with her to Mission. Like Lorenz, Ponds was also in a teacher education program when reforms had gained ascendancy in California. Moreover, both Lorenz and Ponds were in intern programs that combined learning about ideas in the curriculum frameworks with purposeful tasks rooted in classroom teaching. Hence, both teachers brought a prior understanding of instructional practice that was congruent with reforms. Neither teacher had to overcome inherited notions that were in conflict with the reforms. While they continued to learn on the job, neither needed to "unlearn," as did many other staff at Mission.

Finally, Lorenz and Ponds managed with the help of the school leader-ship and state or district policies that supported the teachers' efforts to some extent. For example, the CLAS and the PQR process had the potential to be quite powerful pedagogical tools for teachers such as Lorenz or Ponds. Their practices melded ideas and practical judgments based on classroom particu-lars in a process that was at heart filled with both conflict and creativity.

Coping with Social Conflict

In the case of Alice Michiels and Kate Jones, conflict was a productive change mechanism as well as a force counterproductive to reforms, depending on the degree of capacity that was present. First, Kate Jones may have learned—or opened her mind enough about her teaching to consider changing her practice—because of arguments she was having with her *compañera*, Alice Michiels. The conflict between Jones and Michiels was in the direction of professional interaction, the norm that research and theory suggest can be a resource for learning, as well as a means of accountability. In this instance, a process that included competing ideas, challenge, negotiation, and adjust-ments in belief or practice was productive for Jones where the reforms are concerned (for other examples of the creative potential in norms that feature argument over goals and means, see Little, 1990 or Richarson, 1994).

Moreover, Jones's trial, reform-oriented practices and her students' re-sponse to those practices breached the classroom routine, created cognitive dissonance, and became an incentive for further change. After trying new practices, Jones reported feeling less resistant to the reforms. The discordant change process in the case of Kate Jones was consistent with the idea that "belief can follow action" or "seeing is believing" (Weick, 1979). "Seeing" her students respond to new practices appeared to convince Jones of the reforms' merits. Conflict was productive in these instances because of social and personal resources—that is, the resources residing in the relationship between Jones and Michiels, and Jones's personal comfort with mathematics.

While conflict appeared to be quite productive for curriculum reform in Jones's case, it did not seem especially so in Michiels's case. Competing school and district messages—about the importance of the CTBS and the CLAS results, for example—together with Jones's success in using methods that conflicted with what Michiels was trying to learn, combined to heighten Alice Michiels's ambivalence about her reformed practices. For Michiels, this was not a "safe" context in which to be rehearsing new methods for teaching mathematics. Her practices were challenged but she had only inconsistent support for sustaining them. Her ambivalence between the old reliable practices she had used to build her sense of professional efficacy and the new, untried practices she was working to invent appeared to some degree to undermine her will to progress. With only modest social resources to support the change process, and when change meant giving up some crucial personal resources—such as her sense of efficacy—social conflict was counterproductive to reforms. While conflict fostered change in Jones's practice, without the social support of a guide or mentor, Michiels's conflict with her teammate may have blocked or slowed her progress toward reform.

Further, inconsistent messages and uneven resources made it unlikely that either of these teachers would make deeper or more sustained reform efforts. Social resources at the school were constrained by inherited conceptions of work norms, by the lack of sustained opportunities for these teachers to learn with knowledgeable others, and by the personal resources these two teachers brought to the task of reforming their practices. On the first point, Michiels's interference in Jones's practice was not yet sanctioned by school norms. Further, their discourse did not include a critical mass of reform-oriented teachers in the school. Nor did it tap into the school's subject matter expert. The former would have provided accountability: the pressure of collective staff expectations as a means to judge Jones's or Michiels's personal instructional preferences. The latter could have been the sort of "credible and easily accessible technical assistance" (Elmore & McLaughlin, 1988, p. 46) that researchers report can help teachers change—that is, someone to provide advice on concrete problems of daily practice.

Finally, Jones and Michiels's debate, as a lever for change, was restricted by what these two teachers brought to the task of reform. Each brought only a portion of the capacity they would have needed to change their practices more deeply. Jones was comfortable and capable with mathematics content. But her conception of authority and the nature of mathematical knowledge led Jones to consider learning as a matter of reproducing "the facts," and doing so quickly. Michiels was uneasy with mathematics; she lacked a strong sense of efficacy. But she understood a good deal about cognitive learning theory, her students' background, their thinking, and how to teach them to understand subject matter (in language arts and science). If staff interaction on important issues of practice would have been a routine matter at this school, these teachers might have transformed the differences in what they brought into sanctioned opportunities for learning. The mathematics expert in the school might have been a source of scaffolding for more powerful learning for both teachers. Strong professional norms—norms that held instructional knowledge to be distributed and shared—would have been a rich social resource for deeper change in the case of Michiels and Jones.

In a second instance of social conflict—debates across grade levels—conflict was likely productive for the staff. Juan Ramirez reported a strong sense of efficacy in his instructional capacity and high expectations for his students' achievement. These resources were embedded in the personal and professional identity he brought to the work of reform. Over the course of a year, he challenged kindergarten teachers' assumptions about their teaching goals, and they in turn argued with him, defending their point of view. In this case, conflict, though difficult, appeared to be a productive lever for changing Ramirez's independent work style, due in part to his strong convictions about his students' ability. He became a leader for reform. And by challenging the assumptions of his peers, Ramirez was able to use the personal and professional resources he brought to help invent social resources for the school.

To the extent that conflict challenged tacit assumptions and began to push further toward a culture conducive to staff deliberation on points of practice, such conflict, albeit laced with strong feelings, had the potential to build professional community—common understanding, mutual support for teaching goals, an arena for teaching and learning from one another, and so on. Thus, conflict could be turned to productive purposes for reform and the school. Here Mission's principal, by hiring teachers like Lorenz, Ponds, and Ramirez, who all held very high expectations for their students' academic work, was building a cadre of like-minded change agents at the school—social resources for school improvement.

But another related instance of social conflict at Mission may have been counterproductive to the reform goal of collegiality, and may have damaged the social fabric of the school, thus making collaboration more difficult. In one instance the traditional norm of collective bargaining was pitted against the norm of professional accountability to peers when the loss of individual choice was apparently too costly to some teachers. A few teachers were unwilling to embrace aspects of the norm of "mutual responsibility" for student learning goals—at least initially—because it would have constrained their actions. In this instance, after a series of emotionally charged meetings, several teachers filed a grievance with their union, which then intervened in the matter. The emotional strain and antagonism that lingered after the contentious meetings likely worked counter to the goal of staff collegiality.

Here the process of managing conflict illustrates the double-edged nature of the social relations inherent in rigorous, professional collaboration. On one hand, the counterproductive conflict between kindergarten teachers and the school's leadership was due in part to the lack of collaborative social relations at the school—for example, an established pattern of using public, teacher deliberation as a balancing force on individual choice. According to this view, the staff might have avoided counterproductive conflict had their fledgling attempt at establishing a norm of collective accountability been further along. That norm could have been a social resource for the school, and may have substituted for the clash of authority between the union and management. Laura Mather and her leadership team, as well as the schools' teachers, would have had the forum for productive debate and action.

On the other hand, the conflict was due in part to the staff's attempt to *create* such social relations without any external guidance. From this view, instruction from a veteran of school change, someone knowledgeable about managing the conflict inherent in genuine collaboration, could have helped Laura Mather and the others at Mission. Teachers moving to the public arena of shared goals from the isolation of classroom decision making have a good deal to learn about collaboration, not just as individuals, but as an organization. Trying to envision and then practice behaviors that clash with long-established norms put educators at Mission in the very difficult position of having to step outside their own histories and horizons in order to invent a productive process.

Tensions the Staff Shared

Merging reform principles in practice can be extraordinarily difficult, because while compelling in the abstract, principles can be in tension at the level of practice. Staff had to mange tensions among principles such as clear school-wide goals, complex classroom performances, collaborative norms, primary language instruction, English language instruction, integrated classrooms, and more. Despite the conflicting impulses inherent in such work, it had the potential to build instructional capacity at Mission. But the quality of the work was also influenced by capacity—social and individual resources. For example, contrasting images of Title I instruction after the momentous school-wide plan went into effect illustrated how the call for coherent, school-wide planning worked in tension with the press for more coherent, demanding instruction for Title I children—one of several dilemmas the staff shared. The way in which the staff managed that dilemma produced gains for some teachers and students. But there were also losses. The gains and losses were shaped in part by personal and social resources.

The upper-grade teachers who had sacrificed all their resources for the collective goal of developing students' literacy skills in the early grades had to cope with particular students in their own classrooms who were floundering every day. They managed by reverting to a series of pull-out strategies that appeared to create more fragmented instruction for some Title I students. They thus took an ironic turn away from the 1988 Title I Hawkins-Stafford reform amendments to which they had earlier responded so ambitiously. The new plan was productive for first-grade students and teachers—such as Juan Ramirez and his students. But the tensions embedded in that plan were counterproductive for the upper-grade teachers and students such as Alice Michiels, Kate Jones, and their Title I students.

While there were clearly trade-offs in the new school-wide resource distribution plan, a critical point here is that the value of financial resources—gained and lost under the new school plan—depended in part on personal resources individuals brought to the tasks of teaching children, and on social resources created by staff at the school. So, for example, Juan Ramirez's resource gains were not straightforward. Because his instructional goals clashed to some extent with the beliefs of one assistant he had acquired under the new plan, that particular relationship produced fewer instructional resources than did his relationship with a second assistant he gained. In the latter instance, Ramirez and his Title I teacher held mutually supportive expectations for students. The synergy in their relationship created a substantial instructional resource for the classroom. Conversely, when Alice Michiels lost Monique Ponds, she lost significant personal and social resources that could not be replaced quickly or easily. They had worked together for years and shared a vision of teaching. Ponds had also built personal relationships with the students she had tutored for 2 years. Thus, Michiels and her students sustained a serious loss when they lost Ponds.

PROBLEMS AND OBSTACLES

In all the above-mentioned examples, productive responses did not naturally or spontaneously occur. Managing productively in the face of conflict required determination, learning, and the resources to foster both. For example, Anita Lorenz had rehearsed coping with uncertainty for 3 years in her teacher education program. She had also been challenged and was used to questioning her practice and having others do the same. But for some other teachers at Mission, moving from the isolation and freedom of choice they enjoyed in classrooms to a public arena of debate was a process that people had to learn how to do productively. Likewise, Juan Ramirez and the kindergarten teachers needed time and guidance to learn how to engage in rigorous "joint work" projects. For a while, some staff at Mission were not speaking to one another when they passed in the halls. The staff needed a "teacher" to guide them in their efforts.

Not only does managing conflict require the support of human resources, but it won't be easy to transform conventional or financial resources into the kind of productive instructional resources the reforms seem to expect that schools will somehow have or create. One challenge at Mission was that financial resources for reform were diluted by competing priorities. Generally, funding was sent into a "shopping mall" professional development system based on teacher choice. If most professional development funds had been concentrated on reforms, and if the PQR and CLAS had been the central focus for the school leadership and staff, then the "pedagogy" and "curriculum" of the reform policy could have been a more powerful intervention. But financial resources that were only modest at best were then diluted. Likewise, policy mechanisms to support teachers' learning—the CLAS and the PQR, for example—were weakened by a system that sent inconsistent messages via competing tests, and multiple compelling notions of practice. Thus, teachers at Mission—Kate Jones is one example—had considerable latitude to reject the reforms if they chose to do so.

Another obstacle to converting financial resources into capacity-building resources for reforms was that equivalent funding translated into dramatically different instructional resources, depending on factors such as hiring practices, qualified personnel, long-term relationships, and so on. So personal and social resources shaped in part the extent to which financial resources could be transformed into valuable instructional resources in classrooms. But personal or social resources—individual or collective knowledge, belief, skill, motivation, expectations for student work, and so on—were not easily produced or evenly distributed, even when financial resources were available. Anita Lorenz was able to create instructional resources with her paraprofessional, who was eager to learn and who held the same high expectations for students' work as Lorenz did. But Juan Ramirez reported that the aide he inherited did not take much initiative when working with students, and she disagreed with him about goals. The attitudes and knowledge that this paraprofessional brought to his classroom did not so readily translate into instructional resources. The trust, shared understanding, and mutual expectations that resided in relationships the staff at Mission had created were not interchangeable, and they took time to create. The case of Alice Michiels and Monique Ponds is another example here: They had worked together for several years to build mutual understanding and trust. Personal and social capital shaped the value of the financial losses and gains when it came to instructional resource allocation at Mission.

Furthermore, the social relations (rigorous collaboration that includes interdependent work norms—ongoing conversation, debate, and negotiation over core issues of practice) that according to research and theory have potential to build social resources and capacity for change (for instance, scaffolding for learning, trust, understanding, mutual responsibility for student learning, and agreed-upon goals) were also a source of conflict that worked against collaborative norms at Mission. Similarly, personal histories that in part shaped the staff's response to reform were also a resource for change and could complement reforms. But they also sometimes conflicted with reform goals or became a source of conflict. In either case, teaching is in some respects deeply personal—thus, the difficulty of professional norms in which authority for goals and means is collective and negotiated. Such a norm of "collective accountability" challenges teachers' freedom to choose based on personal preference alone. That is a loss for teachers, as well as a significant, almost revolutionary change in school norms. It is not likely to come easily, no matter the financial support.

Mission's story shows that in an era of both high academic standards and "site-based management," the current, very ambitious reforms have tacitly delegated an enormous amount of responsibility, work, and learning to schools. People who work in them are expected to somehow muster superhuman capacity for complex performances—both the will and the skill. They are to use conceptions of teaching, leading, learning, and school organization that are very different from inherited conceptions. And they are to understand and integrate knowledge from fragmented, contradictory sources, then use it in the action of classroom or school practices.

Thus, while it is very promising that the reforms located the work of improving education for "disadvantaged" children in the schools and classrooms—a middle ground between top-down mandates and the solitary exemplary efforts of individual teachers—it is not realistic to assume that schools and teachers can transform themselves without help. The idea of academic standards for all children, together with school-based management conditioned on collective teacher accountability, has a good deal of merit and potential. But professional collaboration and deliberation over high standards for student learning are also laden with pitfalls. To assume otherwise is a disservice to teachers, administrators, and school leaders. Likewise, to construct "site-based" management as a way to devolve responsibility to schools without a support system in place to help teachers and administrators make sense of frameworks and school-wide strategies seems counterproductive to reform goals.

POSSIBILITIES

The fate of reforms calling for high academic standards for America's children may well depend upon the capacity of school staffs to manage or cope with conflict, and at the same time transform traditional "inputs" into productive instructional resources—that is, personal or social resources. At Mission Elementary, personal or social resources—individual or collective knowledge, belief, skill, motivation, expectations for student work, and so on—also influenced the extent to which financial resources could be transformed into valuable instructional resources. Mission's story shows that when capacity was absent or lacking, conflict was often counterproductive; when it was present conflict could be productive for reform—for individuals as well as the organization. This situation presents a special problem in the U.S. policy system in which conflict and inconsistency are standard fare and in which capacity is most likely to be lacking in those schools most in need of reform.

In Mission, as in so many other schools, inherited ideas about schooling, as well as the social and academic problems, are the primary targets of the reform. But these same ideas and problems limit the capacity of the primary agents of reform—Mission's staff, students, and others like them. Mission's staff was in the difficult position of having to overcome inherited conceptions of teaching, learning, work norms, and school organization in order to enact these unprecedented reforms. But those inherited ideas, what the staff and students brought to the task, and the social and academic problems in the school, limited their capacity to do so. Without authoritative, external guidance, convincing evidence of progress, consistent messages about instructional goals, or other powerful incentives, such a position places an undue burden on school staffs in high-poverty schools.

This view of the problem suggests several avenues for improving schools' response to reforms. Most important is "a new pedagogy" for policy and programs. In order to create a more coherent learning environment for local educators and students, reformers might develop a guidance system that supports a reasonably consistent and stable improvement strategy. Such a system would include a strategy for coordinating instructional goals and measures for schools. Lacking such a system, change advocates might devise a strategy for managing competing demands on schools. Finally, guidance for reforms aimed at changing human practices, beliefs, and knowledge should include a pedagogical infrastructure for adult professionals. Such a structure would include an intelligible curriculum for teachers, teachers of teachers, teachers of leaders or administrators, and a safe environment in which to take the risks involved in maintaining professional responsibilities while seriously engaging in learning new practices.

Reformers could leverage limited financial resources by thoughtfully constructing reform policies to include strong incentives for school districts (or other external entities) to develop instructional systems directed toward reform goals. Developing reform-oriented personal capacity and synergistic social relations—among district and school administrators, teachers, university-based program planners, and other knowledgeable agents of instructional improvement—might transform the allocation of limited funds into something more than a zero-sum game. Over time, capacity for reform could be extended through growing personal resources and productive social relations. Though difficult to create, this kind of capacity building infrastructure would be generative once it was developed. Such an effort would recognize that instructional reforms and new work norms are not small changes for schools to manage: these transformations take time; structural support; and serious, credible instructional support from knowledgeable, experienced professionals.

While the reforms pose tremendous challenges to schools, and while there are no doubt obstacles to overcome, the latest wave of reform rhetoric and action have also created possibilities for progress. This study has pulled apart the policy world of one school in order to examine its competing parts, but it has also provided multiple images of what is possible in schools such as Mission Elementary. Those images offer reformers some reason for optimism. A quick sampling of such images would begin with Gerard, a small boy of Hispanic origin, described by some as illiterate and learning disabled. Imagine you are a visitor to the school—you would see Gerard waving his hand with excitement, aching to respond to a point of discussion in Anita Lorenz's class. His teacher reports his comments were almost always insightful. To her, they count as evidence that he understood a good deal of whatever topic was under discussion. By "listening" to the story others had read, he is able to exercise his judgment, to understand literature, and to participate in the classroom literacy community, while still working on sound-letter correspondence or word recognition. Imagine him poring over his homework pages for hours each evening in the cramped quarters of his home. Take in the walls of Lorenz's classroom covered with children's writing, and graphs of classroom opinions or objects the children had counted, sorted, and displayed. Spend 15 minutes marveling at the deftness with which a second-grade student tutors her Title I classmate on a list of words and their meaning—this "cooperative learning" activity being only one of four or five others taking place in the room where students have learned to help and ask for help.

Or as a visitor you might walk into Kate Jones's classroom as her students (among them a boy living in poverty, whose father was in jail) are giving their accounts of possible rules for predicting numbers in a discussion on patterns. At the end of a long hallway opening to the school's garden, Juan Ramirez's first-grade students might be planting their radishes. On another visit, watch them measure and record the growth of their radishes in journals, then discuss root systems during science class. Or watch small groups of these young children talking about the meaning of poetry and children's literature, leaning over their small table with enthusiasm in order to offer an opinion (and their reasons for it) to the group. Walk over to Monique Ponds's table in a room just down the hall, and observe a small girl, born in the outback of Mexico, crying, wringing her tissue in consternation over a torn paper. Observe as Ponds first consoles her, then guides her quickly back to the task of writing. In the fall of the following school year, this same girl would be standing in front of her classmates reciting poetry over a public address system, poetry that she had earlier discussed with her small group of peers, then illustrated, and finally read aloud herself.

Walk down a covered hallway open to a surrounding view of the foothills, and take in the underwater mural covering one wall. Notice Laura Mather as she speaks in Spanish to her students when they pass. Or think of her offering them pencils on their birthday, and library cards to their parents whenever she has the opportunity. Imagine her sitting day after day in meetings talking about each of her students' academic progress—or lack of it—with teachers and other staff. Wander back out to the school garden and notice the boxes of flowers and vegetables, listening as you do to the tinkling notes of mandolin music coming from room 206. Then observe how teachers throughout the school use the garden to create authentic tasks for students in subjects such as math, science, or language arts. Drop in on Louise James tutoring first graders using Reading Recovery methods. Then follow her as she tutors Monique Ponds on those methods. Listen to the sounds of children chatting in Spanish and English while taking in the full range of skin tones, hair color, and eye color. Enjoy the third-grade English-speaking students as they eagerly take part in a short play directed by Alice Michiels, all in Spanish.

Most of these teachers extended their work lives into the weekend, melding personal and professional spaces: Ramirez volunteered to help students who wanted to participate in the local K-3 race that took place on Saturdays. Another teacher regularly arranged for students to visit his ranch to ride his horses on weekends. Still another was responsible for the music in the school, spending after school and noon-time hours teaching children to play Mariachi instruments. Anita Lorenz organized an art fair for the school. Michiels and Ponds spent many evenings together talking about teaching. Jones spent hours after school and on weekends talking to parents. Mather credits her for helping save a boy who may have been suicidal by alerting and supporting his grandmother. Mather arranged to meet parents on weekends, did fund-raising, or other community work. The staff and students harvested vegetables from the garden and prepared food for the school's parents during evening open houses. There are many more images of what is possible in a school with permeable boarders that permit a flow of activity into the larger, surrounding communal spaces, and the private time of teachers or administrators. This was for the most part a dedicated staff with a good deal of knowledge about their students, their community, and teaching.

But without more structural and instructional help, Mission Elementary's staff may have gone as far as they could toward the reform vision. And they still had a ways to go. Though Mather was trying to invent social resources for change at her school, she was doing so without much institutional support from the district to bolster the rhetoric of "site-based management." At Mission, the state and the district delegated responsibility for achieving "high academic standards" to the school, but not the authority to support school-based accountability. Authority flowed from district management and the union, not from teachers and administrators debating standards of practice. While the staff was struggling to forge new norms that would hold them accountable to one another for mutual goals, they were doing so in a district system with few incentives for sustaining their work. Instructional guidance in the district and state would have been more effective had it capitalized on educators' internal incentives, and created external ones consistent with the reforms' organizational goals (see, for example, Odden, 1996).

Moreover, both teachers and school leaders at Mission Elementary needed extended opportunities to learn a new common language and the conceptual foundation underlying reforms. (See, for example, Carpenter, Fennema, Peterson, Chiang, & Loef, 1989; Richardson, 1994.) Mather, James, Ramirez, Lorenz, Michiels, and a few others were trying to enact radical changes in the school, without much guidance from accessible mentors or role models. That teachers need instructional guidance as they attempt to change their practice is well documented. Guidance must be credible and accessible. But this is so for principals as well, especially in schools trying school-wide reform strategies. The research and theory reviewed in this study together with the story of curriculum reform at Mission Elementary converge on an important point: administrators as well as teachers will need credible and accessible guides to practice—veterans of school-wide change or mentor teachers knowledgeable in subject matter—if reforms are to grow in schools.

Lessons from the field relating specifically to school-wide projects suggest that such reforms "offer the potential for improving learning outcomes of disadvantaged students, but require coordinated and direct support from the central office and district" (Winfield, 1991, p. 353). Winfield found that successful school-wide interventions contained strong pedagogical components, including newly created positions at the district and school levels. People who functioned as teachers or coaches for principals and teachers filled the new positions. These teachers ranged from experienced principals, veterans of school change, to "master teachers." Thus, they were credible sources of help for practicing principals and teachers. In these school-wide projects, instructional frameworks served as a kind of "curriculum" that provided a common language for deliberation among a range of people within the district and schools. While some of the pieces listed here were available at Mission Elementary and the MUSD, some were missing—for example, credible teachers of the reform at the district or school site level who could coach principals and coordinate or manage district demands on schools.

Such guidance for adult professionals could have provided Mission's staff with a curriculum to help them integrate knowledge from across relevant but fragmented domains—for example, learning in a second language and subject matter knowledge. Similarly, a deliberate "pedagogy" for the reforms might have reduced fragmentation in professional development by coordinating development opportunities with the school's instructional goals. Or it might have provided guides to help teachers synthesize information across workshops, coursework, seminars, or other learning opportunities. District or school-based reformers using an explicit "pedagogy" as their strategy could have created more coherent learning environments for adult professionals and students at Mission, either by trying to keep instructional goals and measures consistent, or by otherwise managing competing demands on schools—for example, encouraging schools to prioritize or ignore certain demands in order to pursue coherent instructional goals.

Beyond more coherent environments for learning, a new "pedagogy" for curriculum policy could have created a "safer" environment for adult learning. Change advocates might do this by recasting traditional roles to incorporate serious learning on the job. Reformers might introduce different conceptions of leadership into the work norms of districts and schools, ones in which a leader is also a learner. District office staff, principals, and teachers should have opportunities to learn from one another without the risk of losing the respect of peers, staff, supervisors, or parents. As it stands, the conceptions of leadership, accountability, teaching, and learning raised here entail huge risks for professionals working in schools. The incentives for taking those risks are not as compelling as they might be with more structural "safety nets."

Inventing new roles and the knowledge schools need will also mean that instructional support systems connecting outsiders—state and district offices, university-based improvement facilitators, or other external agents of improvement—with schools must allow for teaching and learning to flow both ways. Administrators, policy planners, program developers, and others throughout the education system could benefit from challenges to their traditional roles and assumptions. These sorts of challenges might best be accomplished through learning opportunities, not only within schools, but extending beyond schools. The staff perspectives in schools such as Mission Elementary hold volumes of important information for district staff, university-based agents of reform, and others. This kind of "connected teaching" system-wide or in smaller subsystems would assume there are reasons for what teachers and administrators in schools do. Likewise, there are reasons for wanting to improve what they do. But conversations are needed that will help integrate the understanding of people working in schools with the understanding of those trying to reform them. Conversations about reform are too often one-sided, didactic, with volumes of advice flowing into schools but few mechanisms in place for schools to "talk back." Though there are various "games"—different interests, functions, and timelines (Firestone, 1989)—within the education system, players can at least try to talk across those games. Reform designers, as well as school leaders; policy planners, as well as teachers will have to converse in an attempt to integrate the knowledge these ambitious reforms need—knowledge that is now distributed across "games." All of us who care about schooling in America could benefit from what Belenky, Clinchy, Goldberger, and Tarule (1986) suggest is a matter of letting the "inside out and outside in" (p. 135).

In California, policy tools such as the CLAS, the PQR process, and replacement units had the pedagogical potential to begin the kind of conversations described just above. The data chapters illustrated that teacher leaders at Mission used the CLAS as a curriculum and teaching tool. Teachers at Mission were creating rubrics based on the frameworks, and their own students' work. This sort of "outside-inside" perspective has the potential to integrate different ways of understanding the work of instructional reform. Mission's teachers used the rubrics they created to score student work and to gain a sense of the kind of performances the CLAS would assess. Cohen and Hill (2001) described similar learning opportunities in California, ones that focused on content (aligned with the assessment) that students study. They found that such opportunities paid off, with higher student scores among those teachers who had participated in them.

Similarly, the PQR process at Mission gave teachers the opportunity to think about what science reform meant at the very specific level of student work in particular classrooms. The process challenged teachers' autonomous decisions to some degree, and it stimulated thinking around a coherent school-wide vision of student work in science. It did this without appearing to cause much conflict. Here was a strategy that entailed teaching, learning, and the negotiation of meaning. Teachers could in one sense "talk back" to the reformers' perspective as they adapted the frameworks' content to particular classrooms. The process was collegial in that it fostered conversation, and seemed to develop common understanding about instructional goals in science. Teachers' assumptions may have been challenged, but because the process did not involve pressing for overt school-wide agreement, those challenges did not seem to have emotional or counterproductive conflict attached to them. Teachers thought about what science reform might look like in their classrooms, but with a mirror held up (via the leadership team) with some concrete examples (model lessons based on the frameworks) and with some concrete materials (their students' work, which had to meet certain specifications). The process integrated an "outside" perspective (frameworks and the leadership team) with teachers' own "inside" perspective. Teachers were working alone or in small groups, but in some respects they were doing so within a common school-wide framework, and thus with a common language for what science meant.

These were the sort of curricular and instructional tools that had the potential to be powerful forces for change at Mission. They were helpful resources and guides in an implementation process where teachers were called upon to invent new, hybrid forms of instruction based on the big ideas in reforms and the particulars in classrooms. But when this study ended, the CLAS was gone, due in part to public and political opposition and in part to technical problems. Furthermore, the new state superintendent's special task force had recommended the PQR be eliminated because it was creating too much paperwork. They wrote that the PQR was "an unnecessary burden to schools."

The demise of the CLAS as well as the pending elimination of the PQR process are but two examples in the very long story of America's episodic attempts at reform within its sprawling, fragmented educational system. In one sense, the ironic turns in Mission's collective response to reforms—toward some elements in the Title I and curriculum reforms, and perhaps at the same time away from other elements in the Title I and curriculum reforms—tell that American story, but from the ground view. Thus, the ironic twists, competing ideals, tensions between levels of activity, personal ambivalence, and social conflict also tell a human story, one infused with passion as well as reason. I have tried to use that story to illustrate something about the nature of education reform in America. That view of reform shows debating and doing are different matters when it comes to a competition of ideas and commitments. The ground view demonstrates some potential, reason for reformers to hope, and some problems or obstacles to the reforms growing in schools. Some of the latter might well give way to remedial pressure and instructional support. But other obstacles—a fragmented education system in a politically contentious environment, for example—seem as solid as "the American way."

Research Procedures and the Data

Generally, my empirical research orientation emerged through my work as part of the Education Policy and Practice Study (EPPS) at Michigan State University and the University of Michigan. The EPPS team investigated mathematics and literacy reforms in a set of classrooms and school districts in three states. My work with EPPS generated some of the broad analytic categories in the data—categories such as teachers' beliefs or attitudes as well as their practices around mathematics reforms, literacy reforms, and so on. That research orientation is part of a long tradition of qualitative research with theoretical underpinnings in the symbolic interaction of the Chicago School of Sociology and the phenomenological approach, in which a researcher attempts to understand her subject's point of view on a topic (Bogdan & Biklen, 1992; Hammersley & Atkinson, 1983/1992).

In the tradition of the theories that emerged from the cognitive revolution sketched in Chapter 1, these research traditions assume that people are actively engaged in creating their own world. Humans interpret and negotiate the meaning of that world in interaction with others and with the help of their past experiences. Thus, the position of teachers and administrators as "learners" or "interpreters" of various reform policies is parallel to the conception of student learners portrayed in the curriculum policies themselves. The method I used is embedded in a larger research tradition that is intellectually consistent with the big ideas that emerged from the cognitive revolution and which informed the reform policies considered here.

In this book, I have also tried to shed light on how ideas and events in a broader social or historical context might compete with, complement, or be mirrored by the meaning that teachers and administrators construct around more current reform ideas. Throughout each data chapter, I used a variety of literature to illustrate debates over "the facts" beyond Mission Elementary.

THE DATA

I observed and interviewed staff at Mission Elementary from January 1993 to June 1995. But I first observed teachers at Mission Elementary in the spring of 1993 as part of the EPPS wave of data collection, in which I sought to learn about categorical programs and the instruction received by "disadvantaged" children in our study's schools. For 2 years, I used interview and observation instruments developed by a subset of our EPPS group—those researchers who were especially interested in the education of "disadvantaged children" or in "diversity" issues. I developed new questions in order to investigate particular issues as they arose in the context of Mission, and I adapted a "life history" protocol to interview teachers about issues that informed their practices (Faraday & Plummer, 1979; Goodson, 1992; Smith, 1994, S. Weiland, personal communication, 1994). But the diversity instruments served as the foundation of my work.

In year 1, I observed Anita Lorenz, Ruth Linn, and Monique Ponds, a Compañero bilingual team of second-grade teachers. Linn taught mostly Spanish-speaking children, Lorenz mostly English-speaking children, and both had many Title I students whom they taught core subjects in their primary language. Monique Ponds, the Title I bilingual teacher who worked part-time in the Spanish-speaking room, was a key subject, because she worked with the handful of students on whose instruction I was focusing in that room. I also observed and/or interviewed a cluster of support staff and school administrators who were in various ways involved with the categorical programs— especially Title I (then Chapter 1)—at the school.

After a year in the second-grade Compañero classrooms, the set of Title I children whose instruction I had been observing were off to another Compañero team for the 1994–1995 school year. I followed the same subset of children to their new third-grade teachers—Alice Michiels and Kate Jones, another Compañero bilingual team—in order to compare the instruction they received that year with instruction of the year before. I continued to observe their instruction as well as interview and "shadow" the school's principal (Laura Mather) and Title I administrator (Louise James). But I added one additional first-grade bilingual teacher to my set of subjects the second year—Juan Ramirez. His room gave me a view into one classroom where three adults were working with first-grade Title I children. This was a "resource-rich" classroom because of a new Title I plan. But the "neediest" Title I children I followed to third grade lost most of their resources because of the new plan.

In all, I focused on eight people: Two second-grade teachers, two third-grade teachers, a bilingual Title I teacher who instructed the Spanish-speaking children in both second- and third-grade classrooms, a first-grade bilingual teacher, the school's principal, and the principal's Title I assistant. In the book chapters, I selected six of the eight people to highlight.

References

Acuña, R. (1988). *Occupied America: A history of Chicanos*. New York: Harper & Row.

Allington, R. L. (1991). Effective literacy instruction for at-risk children. In M. S. Knapp & P. M. Shields (Eds.), *Better schooling for the children of poverty: Alternatives to conventional wisdom* (pp. 9–31). Berkeley, CA: McCutchan.

Anderson, R. C., Hiebert, E. H., Scott, J. A., & Wilkinson, I. A. G. (1985). *Becoming a nation of readers*. Washington, DC: The National Institute of Education.

Au, K. H. (1993). *Literacy instruction in multicultural settings*. New York: Harcourt Brace.

Ball, D. L. (1988). *Research on teaching mathematics: Making subject matter knowledge part of the equation* (Research Report 88-2). East Lansing, MI: Michigan State University, The National Center for Research on Teacher Education.

Ball, D. L. (1991). Teaching mathematics for understanding: What do teachers need to know about subject matter? In M. M. Kennedy (Ed.), *Teaching academic subjects to diverse learners* (pp. 63–84). New York: Teachers College Press.

Baratz, S. S., & Baratz, J. C. (1970). Early childhood intervention: The social science basis of institutional racism. *Harvard Educational Review, 40*, 29–50.

Belenky, M. F., Clinchy, B. M., Goldberger, N. R., & Tarule, J. M. (1986). *Women's ways of knowing: The development of self, voice, and mind*. New York: Basic Books.

Bloom, B. S. (Ed.). (1956). *Taxonomy of educational objectives: The classification of educational goals. Handbook 1. Cognitive domain*. New York: McKay.

Bloom, B. S., Hastings, J. T., & Madaus, G. F. (Eds.). (1971). *Handbook on formative and summative evaluation of student learning*. New York: McGraw-Hill, Inc.

Bogdan, R. C., & Biklen, S. K. (1992). *Qualitative research for education: An introduction to theory and methods* (2nd ed.). Boston: Allyn and Bacon.

Brophy, J. (1983). Classroom organization and management. *Elementary School Journal, 83*, 265–285.

Brophy, J. E. (1991). Effective schooling for disadvantaged students. In M. S. Knapp & P. M. Shields (Eds.), *Better schooling for the children of poverty: Alternatives to conventional wisdom* (pp. 211–235). Berkeley, CA: McCutchan.

Brophy, J., & Good, T. L. (1986). Teacher behavior and student achievement. In M. C. Wittrock (Ed.), *1986 Handbook of research on teaching* (3rd ed., pp. 328–375). Macmillan.

Bruner, J. (1983). *In search of mind: Essays in autobiography.* New York: Harper Colophon Books.

Bruner, J. S. (1990). *Acts of meaning.* Cambridge, MA: Harvard University Press.

Bryk, A. S., Lee, V. E., & Holland, P. B. (1993). *Catholic schools and the common good.* Cambridge, MA: Harvard University Press.

Burlingame, M. (1986, Fall). Using a political model to examine principals' work. *Peabody Journal of Education, 63,* 120-130.

California State Department of Education. (1985). *Mathematics framework for California public schools kindergarten through grade twelve.* Sacramento: Author.

California State Department of Education. (1987a). *English-language arts framework for California public schools.* Sacramento: Author.

California State Department of Education. (1987b). *Mathematics model curriculum guide, kindergarten through grade eight.* Sacramento: Author.

California State Department of Education. (1988). *English-language arts model curriculum guide.* Sacramento: Author.

California State Department of Education, Bilingual Education Office. (1990). *Bilingual education handbook: Designing instruction for LEP students.* Sacramento: Author.

California State Department of Education. (1991). *Mathematics framework for California Public Schools: Kindergarten through grade twelve.* Sacramento: Author.

California State Department of Education, Elementary Grades Task Force. (1992). *It's Elementary!* Sacramento: Author.

California State Department of Education, Complaints Management and Bilingual Compliance Unit of the Bilingual Education Office. (1993). *LEP program guide: Organizing a compliant program for students of limited-English proficiency.* Sacramento: Author.

California State Department of Education. (1995). *A call to action: Improving mathematics achievment for all California students. The report of the California Mathematics Task Force* (0-8011-1245-1). Sacramento: Author.

California State Department of Education. (1995). *Every child a reader. The report of the California Reading Task Force* (0-8011-1244-3). Sacramento: Author.

Carmichael, S., & Hamilton, C. V. (1967). *Black power.* New York: Random House.

Carnegie Forum on Education and the Economy. (1986). *A nation prepared: Teachers for the 21st century. The report of the Task Force on Teaching as a Profession.* New York: Author.

Carpenter, T. P., Fennema, E., Peterson, P. L., Chiang, C. P., & Loef, M. (1989, Winter). Using knowledge of children's mathematics thinking in classroom teaching: An experimental study. *American Educational Research Journal, 26*(4), 499-531.

Cohen, D. K. (1995). *Standards-based school reform: Policy, practice, and performance.* Paper prepared for Brookings Institution conference on performance-based approaches to school reform. Presented at Michigan State University, East Lansing, MI.

Cohen, D. K., & Ball, D. L. (1990). Policy and practice: An overview. *Educational Evaluation and Policy Analysis, 12*(3), 249-256.

Cohen, D. K., & Barnes, C. A. (1993a). Conclusion: A new pedagogy for policy? In D. K. Cohen, M. W. McLaughlin, & J. E. Talbert (Eds.), *Teaching for understanding: Challenges for policy and practice* (pp. 240–275). San Francisco: Jossey-Bass.

Cohen, D. K., & Barnes, C. A. (1993b). Pedagogy and policy. In D. K. Cohen, M. W. McLaughlin, & J. E. Talbert (Eds.), *Teaching for understanding: Challenges for policy and practice* (pp. 207–239). San Francisco: Jossey-Bass.

Cohen, D. K., & Barnes, C. A. (1995, February). *High standards, all children, and learning: Notes toward the history of an idea.* Paper prepared for the Carnegie Corporation of New York, Task Force on Learning in the Primary Grades, New York.

Cohen, D. K., & Hill, H. (2001). *Learning policy: When state education reform works.* New Haven: Yale University Press.

Cohen, D. K., & Spillane, J. P. (1992, Spring). Policy and practice: The relations between governance and instruction. *Review of research in education.* Washington, DC: American Educational Research Association.

Coleman, J. S. (1988, Spring). Social capital in the creation of human capital. *American Journal of Sociology, 94,* 95–120.

Coleman, J. S. (1990). *Foundations of social theory.* Cambridge, MA: Belknap Press, Harvard University Press.

Comer, J. P. (1986). A prescription for better schools: An interview with Dr. James Comer. *CDF Reports, 8*(4), 1–6.

Comer, J. P. (1990). Home, school, and academic learning. In J. I. Goodlad & P. Keating (Eds.), *Access to knowledge: An agenda for our nations' schools.* New York: College Entrance Examination Board.

Chapter 1 Commission. (1992). *Making schools work for children in poverty.* Washington, DC: American Association for Higher Education.

Cuban, L. (1984, January-February). Policy and research dilemmas in the teaching of reasoning: Unplanned designs. *Review of Educational Research, 54,* 665–681.

Cuban, L. (1986, Fall). Principaling: Images and roles. *Peabody Journal of Education, 63,* 107–120.

Cummins, J. (1982). The role of primary language development in promoting educational success for language minority students. In *Schooling and language minority students: A theoretical framework, California State Department of Education.* Los Angeles: Evaluation, Dissemination and Assessment Center, California State University.

Cummins, J. (1989). *Empowering minority students.* Sacramento: California Association for Bilingual Education.

Cusick, P. A. (1983). *The egalitarian ideal and the American high school.* New York: Longman.

Darling-Hammond, L. (1992a). Achieving our goals: Superficial or structural reforms? *Phi Delta Kappan, 72*(4), 286–295.

Darling-Hammond, L. (1992b). Reframing the school reform agenda: Developing capacity for school transformation. *Phi Delta Kappan, 74*(10), 753–761.

Delpit, L. D. (1986). Skills and other dilemmas of a progressive black educator. *Harvard Educational Review, 56*(4), 379-385.

Delpit, L. D. (1988). The silenced dialogue: Power and pedagogy in educating other people's children. *Harvard Educational Review, 58*(3), 280-298.

Dewey, J. (1916/1966). *Democracy and education.* New York: The Free Press.

Dickstein, M. (1977/1989). *Gates of Eden: American culture in the sixties.* New York: Penguin Books.

Dwyer, D. C. (1986, Fall). Understanding the principal's contribution to instruction. *Peabody Journal of Education, 63,* 3-19.

Education Week (in collaboration with the Pew Charitable Trusts). (1997). *Quality counts: A report card on the condition of public education in the 50 states.* (Vol. XVI).

Elmore, R. F., & McLaughlin, M. W. (1988). *Steady work: Policy, practice and the reform of American education* (Report R-3574-NIE/RC). Santa Monica, CA: Rand Corporation.

Faraday, A., & Plummer, A. K. (1979). Doing life histories. *Sociological Review, 27*(4), 773-799.

Firestone, W. A. (1989). Educational policy as an ecology of games. *Educational Researcher, 18*(7), 18-24.

Fullan, M. (1993). *Change forces: Probing the depths of educational reform.* (3rd ed.). London: Falmer Press.

Fullan, M. G., & Stiegelbauer, S. (1991). *The new meaning of educational change.* New York: Teachers College Press.

Gagne, R. M. (1965/1970). *The conditions of learning.* (2nd ed.). New York: Holt, Rinehart and Winston.

Garcia, G., & Pearson, A. D. (1991). Modifying reading instruction to maximize its effectiveness for disadvantaged students. In M. S. Knapp & P. M. Shields (Eds.), *Better schooling for the children of poverty: Alternatives to conventional wisdom* (Vol. II, pp. II-1-16). Menlo Park, CA and Washington, DC: SRI International with Policy Studies Associates.

Gardner, H. (1991). *The unschooled mind: How children think & how schools should teach.* New York: Basic Books.

Glazer, N. (Ed.). (1985). *Clamor at the gates: The new American immigration.* San Francisco: Institute for Contemporary Studies (ICS) Press.

Good, T. (1979). Teacher effectiveness in the elementary school: What we know about it now. *Journal of Teacher Education, 30,* 52-64.

Good, T. L., & Brophy, J. E. (1986). School effects. In M. C. Wittrock (Ed.), *Handbook of research on teaching* (3rd ed., pp. 570-602). New York: Macmillan.

Goodlad, J. I., Soder, R., & Sirotnik, K. A. (Eds.). (1990). *Places where teachers are taught.* San Francisco: Jossey-Bass.

Goodman, K., & Goodman, Y. (1979). Learning to read is natural. In L. Resnick & P. Weaver (Eds.), *Theory and practice of early reading* (Vol. 1, pp. 137-153). Hillsdale, NJ: Erlbaum.

Goodson, I. F. (Ed.). (1992). *Studying teachers' lives.* New York and London: Teachers College, Columbia University.

Greenfield, W. D. (1986, Fall). Moral, social, and technical dimensions of the princi-
palship. *Peabody Journal of Education, 63*, 130-150.
Hakuta, K. (1986). *Mirror of language: The debate on bilingualism*. New York: Basic
Books.
Hammersley, M., & Atkinson, P. (1983/1992). *Ethnography principles in practice*.
London and New York: Routledge.
Heaton, R. M., & Lampert, M. (1993). Learning to hear voices: Inventing a new peda-
gogy of teacher education. In D. Cohen, M. W. McLaughlin, & J. E. Talbert (Eds.),
Teaching for understanding: Challenges for policy and practice. San Francisco:
Jossey-Bass.
Holmes Group. (1990). *Tomorrow's schools: Principles for the design of professional
development schools*. East Lansing, MI: Author.
Jackson, P. W. (1968). *Teachers views, live in classrooms* (pp. 115-155). New York:
Holt, Rinehart, and Winston.
Jenkins, J. R., & Jenkins, L. M. (1987, March). Making peer tutoring work. *Educa-
tional Leadership*, 64-68.
Jennings, N. E. (1996). *Interpreting policy in real classrooms: Case studies of state
reform and teacher practice*: New York: Teachers College Press.
Joncich, G. M. (Ed.). (1962). *Psychology and the science of education: Selected
writings of Edward L. Thorndike*. New York: Teachers College Press.
Kennedy, M. M. (1991). Policy issues in teacher education. *Phi Delta Kappan, 72*(9),
658-665.
Knapp, M. S., & Shields, P. M. (Eds.). (1991). *Better schooling for the children of
poverty: Alternatives to conventional wisdom*. Berkeley, CA: McCutchan Pub-
lishing Corporation.
Lampert, M. (1985). How do teachers manage to teach? *Harvard Educational Re-
view, 55*(2), 178-194.
Lewis, O. (1959). *Five families: Mexican case studies in the culture of poverty*. New
York: BasicBooks. A Division of HarperCollins Publishers.
Lieberman, A., & Miller, L. (1992). *Restructuring schools: What matters and what
works* (NCREST Reprint Series). New York: National Center for Restructuring
Education, Schools, and Teaching. Teachers College, Columbia University.
Lieberman, A., Wood, D., & Falk, B. (1994). *Toward democratic practice in schools:
Key understandings about educational change* (Reprint Series). New York:
National Center for Restructuring Education, Schools, and Teaching. Teachers
College, Columbia University.
Lindblom, C. E., & Cohen, D. K. (1979). *Usable knowledge*. New Haven: Yale Uni-
versity Press.
Lipsky, M. (1980). *Street-level bureaucracy: Dilemmas of the individual in public
services*. New York: Russell Sage Foundation.
Little, J. W. (1990, Summer). The persistence of privacy: Autonomy and initiative
in teachers' professional relations. *Teachers College Record, 91*(4), 509-
536.
Little, J. W. (1993). Teachers' professional development in a climate of educational
reform. *Educational Evaluation and Policy Analysis, 15*(2), 129-151.

Lloyd, D. N. (1978). Prediction of school failure from third-grade data. *Psychological Measurement, 38,* 1193-1200.

Lortie, D. C. (1975). *Schoolteacher: A sociological study.* Chicago: University of Chicago Press.

Madden, N. A., Slavin, R. E., Karweit, N. L., Dolan, L., & Wasik, B. A. (1991). Success for all. *Phi Delta Kappan, 72,* 593-599.

Marris, P. (1974). *Loss and change.* New York: Pantheon Books.

Marris, P., & Rein, M. (1982). *Dilemmas of social reform: Poverty and community action in the United States.* (2nd ed.). Chicago: University of Chicago Press.

McGill-Franzen, A., & Allington, R. (1991). *Flunk 'em or get them classified: The contamination of accountability data.* (Report no. R117E90143). Washington, DC: U.S. Department of Education.

McLaughlin, M. W. (1976). Implementation as mutual adaptation: Change in classroom organization. *Teachers College Record, 77*(6), 339-351.

McLaughlin, M. W. (1987). Learning from experience: Lessons from policy implementation. *Educational Evaluation and Policy Analysis, 9*(2), 171-178.

Mehan, H., Hertweck, A., & Meihls, J. L. (1986). *Handicapping the handicapped: Decision making in students' educational careers.* Stanford, California: Stanford University Press.

Natriello, G., McDill, E. L., & Pallas, A. M. (1990). *Schooling disadvantaged children: Racing against catastrophe.* New York: Teachers College Press.

Newmann, F. M., & Wehlage, G. G. (1995). *Successful school restructuring: A report to the public and educators* (Report no. R117Q00005-95). Madison: University of Wisconsin-Madison, U.S. Department of Education, Office of Educational Research and Improvement, Center on Organization and Restructuring of Schools.

Odden, A. (1996). Incentives, school organization and teacher compensation. In S. H. Fuhrman & J. A. O'Day (Eds.), *Rewards and reform: Creating educational incentives that work* (pp. 226-257). San Francisco: Jossey-Bass.

Odden, A. R. (Ed.). (1991). *Education policy implementation.* New York: SUNY Press.

Odden, A., & Kelley, C. (1997). *Paying teachers for what they know and do.* Thousand Oaks, CA: Corwin Press.

Palincsar, A. S., & Brown, A. L. (1989). Instruction for self-regulated reading. In L. B. Resnick & L. E. Klopfer (Eds.), *Toward the thinking curriculum: Current cognitive research* (pp. 19-40). 1989 Yearbook of the Association for Supervision and Curriculum Development [publisher's data not available].

Pechman, E. M., & Feister, L. (1994). *Implementing schoolwide projects: An idea book.* Washington, DC: United States Department of Education.

Peterson, K. D. (1986, Fall). Vision and problem finding in principals' work: Values and cognition in administration. *Peabody Journal of Education, 63,* 87-107.

Peterson, P. L. (1990). Doing more in the same amount of time: Cathy Swift. *Educational Evaluation and Policy Analysis, 12*(3), 261-281.

Peterson, P. L., & Barnes, C. A. (1996). Learning together: The challenge of mathematics, equity, and leadership. *Phi Delta Kappan, 77*(7), 485-492.

Peterson, P. L., Fennema, E., & Carpenter, T. (1991). Using children's mathematical knowledge. In B. Means, C. Chelemer, & M. S. Knapp (Eds.), *Teaching advanced skills to at-risk students: Views from research and practice* (pp. 68-102). San Francisco: Jossey-Bass.

Pinnell, G. S. (1990, September). Success for low achievers through Reading Recovery. *Educational Leadership*, 17-21.

Porter, A. C. (1991). Good teaching of worthwhile mathematics to disadvantaged students. In M. S. Knapp & P. M. Shields (Eds.), *Better schooling for the children of poverty: Alternatives to conventional wisdom* (pp. 125-149). Berkeley, CA: McCutchan.

Purkey, S. C., & Smith, M. S. (1983). Effective schools: A review. *The Elementary School Journal, 83*(4), 427-452.

Purkey, S. C., & Smith, M. S. (1985). School reform: The district policy implications of the effective schools literature. *The Elementary School Journal, 85*(3), 353-389.

Raftery, J. R. (1992). *Land of fair promise: Politics and reform in Los Angeles Schools, 1885-1941*. Stanford: Stanford University Press.

Ravitch, D. (1983). *The troubled crusade: American education, 1945-1980*. New York: Basic Books.

Resnick, L. B., Bill, V. L., Lesgold, S. B., & Leer, M. N. (1991). Thinking in arithmetic class. In C. Chelemer, B. Means, & M. S. Knapp (Eds.), *Teaching advanced skills to at-risk students*. San Francisco: Jossey-Bass.

Resnick, L. B., & Klopfer, L. E. (1989). Toward the thinking curriculum: An overview. In L. Resnick & L. Klopfer (Eds.), *Toward the thinking curriculum: Current cognitive research*. 1989 Yearbook of the Association for Supervision and Curriculum Development [no publisher's data available].

Resnick, L. B., & Resnick, D. P. (1989). Assessing the thinking curriculum: New tools for educational reform. In B. R. Gifford & M. C. O'Connor (Eds.), *Future assessments: Changing views of aptitude, achievement, and instruction*. Boston: Kluwer Academic Publishers.

Richards, J. J. (1991). Commentary: Using children's mathematical knowledge. In C. Chelemer, B. Means, & M. S. Knapp (Eds.), *Teaching advanced skills to at-risk students: Views from research and practice* (pp. 102-112). San Francisco: Jossey-Bass.

Richardson, V. (Ed.). (1994). *Teacher change and the staff development process: A case in reading instruction*. New York: Teachers College Press.

Riessman, F. (1962). *The culturally deprived child*. New York: Harper Row.

Rowan, B., Guthrie, L., Lee, G., & Guthrie, G. P. (1986). *The design and implementation of Chapter 1 instructional services: A study of 24 schools*. (Contract no. 400-85-1015). San Francisco: Office of Educational Research and Improvement, U.S. Department of Education, Far West Laboratory for Educational Research and Development.

Scott, W. R. (1992). *Organizations: Rational, natural and open systems*. (3rd ed.). Englewood Cliffs, NJ: Prentice Hall.

Slavin, R. E., Karweit, N. L., & Wasik, B. A. (1991). *Preventing early school failure: What works?* Baltimore: Johns Hopkins University, Center for Research on Effective Schooling for Disadvantaged Students.

Slavin, R. E., & Madden, N. A. (1991). *Modifying Chapter I program improvement guidelines to reward appropriate practices.* Baltimore: Johns Hopkins University, Center for Research on Effective Schooling for Disadvantaged Students.

Smith, L. M. (1994). Biographical method. In N. K. Denzin & Y. Lincoln (Eds.), *Handbook of qualitative research* (pp. 286–305). Thousands Oaks, CA: Sage.

Snow, C. E. (1992). Perspectives on second-language development: Implications for bilingual education. *Educational Researcher, 21*(2), 16–19.

Sykes, G. (1990). Fostering teacher professionalism in schools. In R. F. Elmore & Associates (Eds.), *Restructuring schools: The next generation of educational reform* (pp. 59–97). San Francisco: Jossey-Bass.

Thorndike, E. L. (1912). *Education: A first book.* New York: The Macmillan Company.

Turnbull, B. J. (1990). *What is "success" in Chapter I?* Washington, DC: Policy Studies Associates.

United States Department of Education. (1994, November). *Chapter 1 handbook* (Vol. XV, No. 3). Washington, DC: Author.

Webb, N. L. (1993). Mathematics education reform in California. In *Science and mathematics education in the United States: Eight innovations* (Vol. 1, pp. 117–143). Paris, France: Organization for Economic Co-operation and Development.

Weick, K. E. (1979). *The social psychology of organizing.* (2nd ed.). New York: McGraw-Hill.

Wilson, S. M. (1991). A conflict of interests: The case of Mark Black. *Educational Evaluation and Policy Analysis, 12*(3), 309–326.

Winfield, L. F. (1991). Lessons from the field: Case studies of evolving schoolwide projects. *Educational Evaluation and Policy Analysis, 13*(4), 353–362.

Zucker, A. A. (1991). Review of research on effective curriculum and instruction in mathematics. In M. S. Knapp & P. M. Shields (Eds.), *Better schooling for the children of poverty: Alternatives to Conventional Wisdom.* Berkeley, CA: McCutchan.

Index

About the Author

Carol A. Barnes has 16 years of experience in public policy: first as a policy advisor at the state and federal levels of government, and, for the past 8 years, as a university-based researcher. Her research has focused on how educational policy is put into practice in high-poverty schools and classrooms. She is currently an assistant research scientist at the University of Michigan and an associate director of the Study of Instructional Improvement, a national, multi-year study of how school reform programs impact instruction. Her interests in research include the macro and micro influences on school renewal in high-poverty settings, especially the pedagogical aspects of policy implementation and the role of learning as a lever for complex change.